Declaration

In accordance with the decrees issued by Pope Urban VIII, the editors of these revelations declare that they submit themselves to the judgment of the Holy See.

In the A.A.S. 58/16 of 1966-12-29, was published a decree of the Congregation for the Doctrine of the Faith, approved by H.H. Pope Paul VI on the 1966-10-14, according to which the articles 1399 and 2318 of Canon Law were annulled. It is permitted since then to publish, without an imprimatur, texts relating to new revelations, apparitions, prophecies or miracles, without compromising the Holy Roman Catholic Church in any way.

Mary, Queen of Peace, stay with us

Testimonies in favor of Medjugorje

Father Guy Girard
Father Armand Girard
Father Janko Bubalo

Éditions Paulines — Maison St-Pascal

Originally published as

Marie, Reine de la Paix, demeure avec nous

by Éditions Paulines, Montreal, Canada.

Description of the cover page.

New fruits bearing the colors of heaven and the fragrance of Faith are being offered to Mary. The exceptional beauty of the photograph creates an atmosphere of silence and contemplation. Against an earthy-brown background, the cross rises bright with the colors of the Rainbow. Of the body of Jesus nailed to the cross, we see the arms outstretched in a gesture of offering. The infinite suffering of God escapes our human sight and, yet, light illuminates the cross and the Crucified. The color sequence of violet to blue, of yellow to red, show the suffering heart of Jesus and of his Mother already opening out to the Resurrection. The truth of the cross is rooted in the Golgotha. By it, God reveals his irresistible love and offers humanity an authentic promise of Life. The Rainbow, with its delicate range of colors, recalls the discreet presence of Mary at the foot of the cross, in her role as Mother. She is the "Gate of heaven". The earthy-brown reveals the complexity of the history of humanity torn between anguish and hope. The most delicate blending of the suffering of the cross into the light of the Rainbow reflects the fidelity of God the Father to mankind in the sacrifice of his Son.

Christ, Our Savior, remains the central point between heaven and earth while Mary, the Queen of peace, reveals her message of sacrifice, prayer and love in order to help the people who fall and who seek to rise again.

Phototypesetting: *Les Éditions Paulines*

Cover: *Antoine Pépin*

ISBN 2-89039-187-6 (Éditions Paulines)
ISBN 2-9801070-0-1 (Maison St-Pascal)

Legal deposit: 3rd quarter 1988
Bibliothèque nationale du Québec
National Library of Canada

© 1988 Les Éditions Paulines
       250, boul. St-François Nord
       Sherbrooke, QC, J1E 2B9

       Maison St-Pascal
       3719, boul. Gouin Est
       Montréal, QC, H1H 5L8

We dedicate this book

To Mary Queen of Peace

To our spiritual Mother

*To our own beloved mother
who has prayed so much to Mary*

*To all those who love Mary
and whom She calls "My dear children"*

Contents

PART THREE

PART FOUR

PART FIVE

PART SIX

Introduction

While reading the separate testimonies on Medjugorje written by the twin brothers, Canadian priests of the Society of the Holy Apostles (Société des Saints Apôtres or S. SS. A.) of Montreal, the overpowering words of Psalm 19 echo in my mind: "No speech or words are used, no voice is heard, but to all the world, their message is heard to the ends of the earth" (Ps 19:3-4). The Girard brothers were unable to resist this voice; they answered the call and followed it as millions of others had done before them.

Thus, challenged by this "invitation", the brothers, Armand and Guy Girard, went even as far as Medjugorje. This was after a retreat for priests in Rome, a retreat which had brought together, in one and the same spirit, six thousand priests and about one hundred bishops and archbishops from all over the world. But, "a city built on a hilltop cannot be hidden" (Mt 5:14). Thus, the Girard brothers, in their openness to the Spirit, could not help seeing another basilica "not built by men", as one of them said, where the divine kindness and the grace of joy are displayed in a special way. Yes, they went on and they reached Medjugorje.

In these pages, you will discover the enthusiasm and the experiences they had. You will also find out that, having spent a few days in this "Blessed Land", as they labeled this place, the Girard brothers were on their way back to Canada via Italy when, having reached Split, they were unable to resist the urge to go back to Medjugorje and allow themselves to be more imbued by its "rays from the sun" in order to relay these rays to others.

They were truly filled with this light and they could not help spreading it. Once in Canada again, together they wrote a booklet entitled *Medjugorje, Terre bénie*. Their testimony was so spontaneous and warm that this little book was quickly distributed and sold, and it achieved a sizeable circulation. The fact that we are now offering the English version of the Croatian edition is not mere chance. Furthermore, this book is completed by an honest and sincere description of a Canadian mystic of Montreal, Georgette Faniel, servant of the Eternal Father, who, since the age of six (she is now 73), hears the voice of speakers from heaven with whom she regularly converses. Georgette is a mysterious martyr who offers all her life of suffering, physical, moral, spiritual and intimate, to the Eternal Father. For the last four years, according to the explicit wish of the Eternal Father, she has been offering her suffering to the Lord so that the *authenticity* of the apparitions of Our Lady of Medjugorje may be recognized.

The Girard brothers again spent some ten days in Medjugorje in mid-October 1986. This stay was yet richer in experiences and brought them much fruit. They were particularly happy when they learned that their book was being published in the Croatian language. They are true apostles of the Queen of Peace, for they have recognized in Mary, the Mother, the Protector and the Mediatrix of mankind. They have become her most fervent preachers. Precious are the messengers of the Good News proclaiming peace and salvation (Is 52:7) as do the Girard brothers of the Society of the Holy Apostles of Montreal, Canada.

All this will become obvious as you read this book which we present to you.

Janko Bubalo

Part One

Medjugorje

Medjugorje is a tiny village hidden in the mountains of Yugoslavia. It is located in the Croatian Catholic region of Herzegovina. It has almost become universal. People of all conditions have visited it and are still going there. This small village is now known internationally. What has made the whole world turn towards Medjugorje?

The Apparitions

What has happened and what is still happening (as of May 1988) is that the Blessed Virgin Mary is appearing. Beginning on June 24, 1981, the Virgin Mary has appeared every day with five exceptions to six teenagers (4 girls, 2 boys). Their first names, birth dates and current ages (1988) are:

Vicka, born September 3, 1964, 24 years old,
Mirjana, born March 18, 1965, 23 years old,
Marija, born April 1, 1965, 23 years old,
Ivan, born May 25, 1965, 23 years old,
Ivanka, born June 21, 1966, 22 years old,
Jakov, born March 6, 1971, 17 years old.

What puzzles several theologians is the duration and the frequency of the apparitions. Over the last 83 months, the Virgin Mary has appeared more than 2,000 times and the apparitions are still going on. It seems to us that the reason for the duration and the frequency of the Blessed Virgin's apparitions is the importance of Her requests, Her messages and Her secrets.

The Requests of the Blessed Virgin

The most important request of the Virgin Mary is contained in the Croatian word MIR, which means PEACE in English. It has appeared in glowing letters above the hill where the cross stands. Father Jozo and some villagers have witnessed it. The Virgin Mary speaks of peace, of an outright peace which comes from the heart. The roots of this peace are: conversion and faith, daily prayer, fasting and the sacrament of Reconciliation.

Conversion and Faith

This outright conversion, which She insists upon so strongly, is very demanding. The Blessed Virgin knows it and yet requests this for our salvation. This means much more than simply believing in a Superior Being. It involves more than weekly Mass and the reception of the sacraments. This deep conversion is a return to Jesus, our Lord and Savior, which goes beyond all understanding and is found through faith in one's heart. It is a daily encounter with Jesus which transforms our life and grows in importance through FAITH, increasingly nourished by daily prayer, and the Holy Eucharist.

On April 26, 1983, Our Lady said: "Do not wait... I am asking for conversion. Be prepared for anything and be converted. Renounce everything which is a barrier to conversion." The Virgin Mary is calling on each one of us. She is calling not only on those who deal directly with God, but also on the "casual" Christians, who are doing only the minimum. She is also calling on priests, all religious orders and laity.

14

Daily Prayer

Mary presents herself to the visionaries as a person of prayer, and insists on a return to daily prayer. "Many believers don't pray and faith cannot exist without prayer." Life has now become a prayer at Medjugorje. The Blessed Virgin prays with the visionaries. Parishioners and pilgrims pray at least three hours a day, including the celebration of Mass. An entire Christian community is challenging us. They are living a life of prayer. The Blessed Virgin has asked us to recite the Apostles' Creed (the "I believe in God") to tell our Heavenly Father what we believe in, and She has asked us to recite seven "Our Fathers", "Hail Marys" and "Glory be to the Fathers". She stresses the importance of reciting the Rosary daily and even more, the full 15 decades.

Concerning Mass, the Virgin Mary says: "The Mass is the best prayer to God, and you will never be able to understand its greatness; therefore, you must be humble and perfect during Mass, and prepare yourselves well for it". This invitation of the Blessed Virgin Mary should lead us to deep thought and meditation. How many Christians have skipped Mass! How many are attending Mass only at Christmas and Easter as a part of folklore! How many are attending Mass only when they "feel" a need for it, as if the faith were a matter of feelings. Mary says and repeats: "I am asking for conversion. Be prepared for anything and BE CONVERTED. *Renounce everything which is a barrier to conversion.*"

Prayer is a way of communicating with God and uniting ourselves with the Virgin Mary. Prayer is just as important for life in God as air is necessary for breath and life. Because of its obedience to the Blessed Virgin's requests, Medjugorje has become a unique meeting place of prayer. For more than 83 months, this Christian community has been praying from 3 to 4 hours a day; it sends an urgent message to the modern world: "Listen to and obey the requests of the Virgin Mary". They received this message from the Heart of Mary, and they have a responsibility to communicate it to us. On our answer depends our own salvation and the salvation of the whole world.

Fasting

Mary has clearly recommended the best way to fast, i.e. bread and water. Fasting means nothing by itself. It serves only to promote Faith. Fasting is a better way to dedicate our life to God and to others. It cannot be replaced. The Blessed Virgin told the visionaries: "Christians have forgotten that fasting and prayer are powerful enough to stop a war and even natural disasters". Prayer and charity do not replace fasting. Fasting is an opportunity to change ourselves and the whole of humanity. Fasting, like constant prayer, is the most reliable means of conversion. One day, the disciples came to Jesus and asked him: "Why couldn't we drive the demon out?" (Mt 17:19). To this Jesus answered: "Only prayer and fasting can drive this kind out, nothing else can" (Mt 17:21).

Mary wishes that all believers, except the sick, fast every Friday on bread and water. I know some families as well as students that are fasting and they are already feeling a change in themselves.

The Sacrament of Reconciliation

The Sacrament of Reconciliation has almost disappeared from our lives. The Blessed Virgin describes it as a cure for the Western Church. "Whole sections of the Church would be healed if believers went to confess their sins once a month." Pastoral experiences has proved beyond doubt that Reconciliation not only confirms God's Mercy, but also brings psychological and physical healing. Without denying the role of psychiatrists, how many patients would be healed if they had recourse to this sacrament? Unfortunately, psychiatry excludes the supernatural dimension of man from all treatment. Pope John Paul II said once again at Jarry Park, Montreal, Canada: "The human heart does not get accustomed to the absence of God".

The Sacrament of Reconciliation gives us an interior peace, which comes from the Holy Spirit and leads to Peace with our brothers and sisters, Peace within our nation, and Peace around the world.

Those briefly stated are the main requests of the Virgin Mary. Father Tomislav Vlasić said to the 200 priests gathered at Medjugorje on October 13, 1984: "Deepen your FAITH, pray constantly, fast, receive the Sacrament of Reconciliation; these are the requests of the Blessed Virgin Mary". Pray and let God bring about the results. It is easier for us to pray. Action is God's business, while prayer is our business. Only God can bring about the results.

The Messages

Messages and secrets are different. Messages are given by the Blessed Virgin to the visionaries. They are for the parish of Medjugorje, for the Church of Yugoslavia, and for the world. Many messages have been given, and 171 have been recorded so far. A translation from Croatian to English has been made[1].

During the 10 days we spent in Medjugorje, some messages were given. Here is the message given to the 200 priests on October 13, 1984: "My very dear sons, today my son Jesus has allowed me to bring you together here to give this message to you and to all those who love me. My very dear sons, pray constantly and ask the Holy Spirit to inspire you always. In all your requests and in all your actions, have only one desire, to accomplish basically the Holy will of God. My very dear sons, thank you for having answered my call". Here is another message given to Marija on October 18, 1984: "Tell the people to read the Bible each day, especially the New Testament, and place it where it can be seen at any time". Much more could be said about the messages, but these were brought up only to spark interest in the reader. Messages were given every week from March 1, 1984 to January 8, 1987. The Virgin Mary now gives a message on the 25th of each month.

A message was given to Mirjana in Sarajevo on January 28, 1987. It is exceptional in the sense that the Virgin Mary speaks of the SECRETS for the first time. She then comes back to her great requests: peace, conversion, rosary, sacrament of Reconciliation, fasting. She warns us against the influence of Satan.

---

1. See PART IV, page 113.

The extraordinary apparition of Mary, Queen of Peace, to Mirjana on January 28, 1987.

"My dear children,

I have come to lead you to purity of the soul and, thereby, to God. How have you accepted me? In the beginning, with disbelief, fear and distrust towards the children whom I had chosen. Then, most received me in their heart and began to carry out my motherly requests. But, unfortunately, this did not last very long. Wherever I manifest myself, and with me my Son, Satan turns up also. You have allowed him to control and guide you without your being aware of it. You are sometimes aware that your behavior is against the law of God, but you quickly suppress this awareness. Do not give in, my children. Dry away the tears in my face, tears that I shed when I see how you behave. Look at what is going on around you!

Take time to come closer to God in the church. Come to the house of your Father.

Take time to get together as a family and pray for the grace of God.

Remember your deceased. Rejoice them through the Mass.

Do not scorn the poor who begs you for a crust of bread. Do not refuse him the overabundance of your meals. Help him and God will also help you. Perhaps the blessing[1] which he gives you in thanksgiving will come true for you. Perhaps God will hear him. You have forgotten all that, my children. Satan has influenced you in that respect. Do not yield to him! Pray with me! Do not delude yourselves by thinking: "I am good but my brother, who lives near me, is not." You would not be right in doing so. I love you because I am your Mother and that is why I am warning you.

There are some secrets, my children! And you do not know what they are; but when they will be known, it will be late! Go back to prayer! Nothing is more necessary than prayer! I would have liked the Lord to let me enlighten you at least a little on the secrets, but He is already offering you enough graces. Reflect on

---

1. In Croatia, the poor who receives will say "God bless you" instead of "Thank you".

this! How much do you, yourselves, offer to Him? When was the last time you gave up something for the Lord?

I do not wish to reprimand you anymore, but I want to call you once again to prayer, to fasting and to penance. If you wish to obtain the grace of God through fast, then let no one know that you are fasting. If you wish to obtain the grace of God by giving alms to the poor, let no one know you are doing so except yourself and the Lord. Listen to me, my children!

Meditate in prayer this message which I am giving you."

N.B. The apparition lasted about ten minutes.

The Secrets

The secrets are given to the visionaries only. They cannot be transmitted without the approval of the Blessed Virgin. All the visionaries know the date when the secrets will be revealed. There are 10 secrets. They were revealed gradually by the Blessed Virgin. In August 1987, we knew how many secrets were known by each of the visionaries. MIRJANA and IVANKA knew 10 of them, VICKA, MARIJA, IVAN and JAKOV, 9.

These secrets deal with impending disasters and how to mitigate them. We know that one of the secrets relates to a great sign that the Blessed Virgin will leave at the place of the first apparition. *This sign will be visible and permanent. Even non-believers will not be able to deny it.* However, we do not know what this sign will be, nor when it will occur. Mirjana says that the sign will *command attention*. She adds: "Most of the secrets are depressing, but they must not instill fear in us. Our Lord made me understand that. Mary is with us. If we accept her as our Mother, God as our Father and Jesus as our Brother, this family will not fail us."

"Convert quickly", said the Blessed Virgin, *"and do not wait for the sign which has been announced. For the nonbelievers, it will be too late to be converted."* She puts particular emphasis on daily prayer (Mass as often as possible), penance, fasting, conversion (the Sacrament of Reconciliation) and deep faith. These are the ways to prepare for the events which have been

foretold, says the Virgin Mary. The Blessed Virgin said to Mirjana: "Three days before the fulfilment of each secret, you will then be allowed to reveal this secret to a priest of your choice". Mirjana has chosen Father Petar Ljubicić to divulgue the secrets. He will fast 10 days on bread and water. On the seventh day he will reveal the secret Mirjana will have told him and, three days later, the foretold event will come about.

Mirjana says that the Blessed Virgin handed her a plain piece of paper on which the ten secrets are written. One cannot describe the material used for this sheet of paper. "The writing is not visible", Mirjana tells us. "At the right moment, I will hand over the paper to the priest I have chosen. He will receive the grace to read only the first secret; he will read the others later."

This priest will be free to choose the appropriate way to divulge the secrets. For instance, he could transmit these secrets to someone in writing, and they would be published only after the occurrence of the said events. He could also warn the people through the media, by saying something like: "Here is what is going to happen...". The secrets will be gradually revealed so that the people will realize that the apparitions of the Blessed Virgin were authentic.

In a letter sent to the Pope, Mirjana says: "Before the visible sign is shown to humanity, three warnings will be given to the world. These warnings will refer to events which will take place on earth. Mirjana will witness these events. Three days before one of the admonitions, she will inform a priest freely chosen of the forthcoming event. The testimony of Mirjana will be a confirmation of the apparitions and will be an incentive to world conversion".

After the admonitions, the visible sign will be given for humanity on the site of the apparitions at Medjugorje. The sign will be given as evidence of the apparitions and as a call to faith.

The 9th and 10th secrets are very serious. They are a punishment for the sins of the world. The punishment is unavoidable, as we cannot expect the conversion of the whole world. Prayers and penance can alleviate the punishment; however, the latter cannot be avoided. According to Mirjana, the 7th secret, which was announcing a threat for the world, is mitigated because of prayer and fasting. For this reason, the Blessed Virgin continues to urge us to pray and fast.

After the first admonition, the others will follow in a relatively short period of time. Thus, humanity will have time to become converted. This time is the period of grace and conversion. *"After the visible sign, the survivors will hardly have any time left for conversion."*

Father Tomislav asked Mirjana if the last secret could be avoided. To this she answered: "People must prepare themselves spiritually and be ready for anything; they must not panic and should reconcile themselves inwardly. They should be ready for everything, even to die tomorrow". With deep faith and firm belief in reconciliation with God, people must not be afraid, for God is with them. That means total conversion and complete commitment to God. To the question asked in 1986 "Why is it taking so long to divulge the secrets?", she replied that this is a "merciful delay" on the part of God.

The Signs

Visible signs have been seen by some parishioners of Medjugorje and some pilgrims. We mention four of them which have been confirmed.

As at Fatima, the sun danced more than once. It started to rotate around its axis. It was getting closer to the pilgrims, and then bounce back. This sign was seen by almost one hundred and fifty persons on August 2, 1981 (Feast of our Lady of the Angel).

A column of light often appears on the mountain of Krizevac, also called the mountain of the cross. Some people have seen a luminous female figure on top of the hill. Some witnesses assert that they have seen these phenomena on several occasions, and at different times of day. Similarly, people talk about a fire that burnt suddenly at the end of October 1981 on the hill of the apparitions. Many pilgrims witnessed this event. The police officer who was stopping people at the bottom of the hill went up and checked, but could not find any sign of a fire nor ashes. On that day, the Blessed Virgin said to the visionaries: "It is one of the preliminary signs of the great sign. All these signs are given to strengthen your faith until I send the permanent sign".

We should also recall that the Croatian word MIR (PEACE) has been seen written in the sky. According to the visionaries, the Blessed Virgin has promised that there would be many other preliminary signs in Medjugorje and in other parts of the world before the great sign appears.

Presentation of the Visionaries

It appears necessary to me to provide some information on each of the visionaries at this time (May 1988). There are frequent rumors suggesting that the apparitions have ceased, that the Virgin Mary does not give any more messages, that She now appears but once a month, etc.

Together let us now meet the visionaries.

Mirjana

She is studying at the University of Sarajevo and she turned 23 on March 18, 1988. The Virgin Mary appeared to her every day until December 25, 1982. On that day, she was told the tenth secret. The Blessed Virgin told her that She would appear to her every year on her birthday, but we know that the apparitions to her have recurred occasionally to prepare the end of the apparitions.

Ivanka

She was told the tenth secret on May 7, 1985. She, therefore, does not see the Blessed Virgin anymore, except on the anniversary of the apparitions on June 25 of each year. She was 22 on June 21, 1988. On December 28, 1986, she married a young villager of Medjugorje. The Virgin Mary spoke to her of the PAST and of the FUTURE of the CHURCH. On June 25, 1987, the Virgin Mary appeared to her in her home. The ecstasy lasted ten minutes. Father Laurentin was present as well as Mrs. Daria Klanac.

Vicka

She was told the ninth secret on April 22, 1986. On April 10, 1985, the Virgin Mary completed the account of Her own life which She had related over a period of 825 days (three manuscripts). This account of Her life was not dictated. It is important to understand that. On the next day, April 11, 1985, Vicka was told the name of the priest who will publish this "Life of the Blessed Virgin", but his name remains unknown for the time being. On April 23, 1986, the Virgin Mary brought the messages on the FUTURE OF THE WORLD to a close. It is important to understand that.

In 1986, the Virgin Mary discontinued her apparitions to Vicka on three different occasions, that is, from January 6 to February 25, from April 25 to June 4 and from August 25 to October 20. In 1988, Vicka was subjected to a fourth interruption, that is, from January 9 to February 29. Fathers Guy and Armand Girard, S.SS.A., were witnesses to the apparition of October 20, 1986. It occurred at Vicka's home and the ecstasy lasted 10 minutes. Mrs. Daria Klanac was also present.

Vicka suffers much physically. She says: "When this rust attacks us, we must not allow ourselves to be corroded. With love, we can always keep on smiling." Actually, most of the apparitions of the Virgin Mary to Vicka take place in her home. The apparition occurs daily and is prolonged.

Marija

She knows nine secrets. She is a hairdresser by trade, but lives with her parents in order to work with them in the tobacco fields and the vineyard. She takes care of her brother's children. The Virgin Mary appears to her every day. She is the one who received the Thursday messages and who now receives the message given once a month on the 25th. (These messages are addressed to the parish, to the Church and to the world.)

Her intimacy with Mary grows more and more. When these daily apparitions cease, she will enter a convent. Milka, Marija's sister, saw the Virgin Mary only once, on June 24, 1981. To a question asked by a priest concerning the lapse of time since the apparition, Milka replied: "But five years for me is like yesterday."

Ivan

He was 23 on May 25, 1988. Nine secrets have been revealed to him. He completed his military service in June 1987. At the military base, he had inner messages (he could hear the voice of the Virgin Mary in his heart). The Virgin Mary would appear to him when he was not at the military base. Now that he is at Medjugorje, the Virgin Mary appears to him everyday as she does to the other visionaries (Marija, Vicka, Jakov).

Jakov

Jakov was 17 on May 6, 1988. He is the youngest of the visionaries. His father and mother passed away during the period of the apparitions. The Virgin Mary has ceased speaking to him about the FUTURE OF THE WORLD. He is studying to become a "locksmith"; his plans to become a priest are not entirely set aside. Considering his age, he needs to think out this choice thoroughly. He is now an autonomous and very brilliant adolescent. The Virgin Mary appears to him every day.

Commissions of Theological Studies

A new commission was appointed at the level of the Yugoslav Episcopal Conference to study the apparitions of the Blessed Virgin at Medjugorje. It consists of 12 members. This decision was taken in conjunction with the Congregation for the Doctrine of the Faith whose president is Cardinal Ratzinger. We recall that the first commission was dissolved on May 2, 1986 at the request of this same Congregation.

The Medical Commissions

A French medical commission under the direction of Doctor Henri Joyeux and consisting of several specialists has produced a substantial scientific report which is very favorable to Medjugorje. Another Italian medical commission under the direction of Doctor Marco Margnelli consisting of twelve Italian physicians divided into three teams of four has equally submitted a very positive scientific report. Doctor Margnelli (an agnostic) had studied the phenomenon of ecstasy in the context of psychiatry. Subsequently to his expert evaluations at Medjugorje, he is now questioning his faith for, according to him, the ecstasies are authentic.

These two teams met in Milan at the place of Doctor FARINA, president of the ARPA. There were also some theologians present. They reached common and positive conclusions. These conclusions and the records of the Italian physicians were handed over to the Holy Father John Paul II. He acknowledged the reception of them and transferred these reports to the Congregation for the Doctrine of the Faith.

An interview with the Visionaries

Now, by means of questions and answers, we want to tell you what was said to the visionaries.

1. *What does the Blessed Virgin say about the hereafter?*

Four of the visionaries have seen hell and have been told by the Blessed Virgin: "This is the punishment for those who don't want to believe in God. Many go to hell; this is the punishment of the unfaithful". Many do not believe that the devil exists and rather speak of the forces of evil as being esoteric. However, the devil is a being who wants our damnation and fights against God. All the visionaries have seen heaven. The Blessed Virgin says that a very small minority go directly to heaven nowadays. Most of the people go to purgatory because they die without being prepared; they are not ready to accept God and his grace.

2. How could a God, who is so merciful, lack mercy to the point of sending someone to hell for all eternity?

People who go to hell do not love God. Moreover, they hate Him and curse Him more than ever. They become a part of hell and they do not think about their own salvation.

3. Has the Blessed Virgin shown you purgatory?

Yes, She told me: "There are several levels in purgatory. There is the lowest level, where souls are closest to hell, and then, there are intermediate levels which get closer to heaven. These souls are waiting for your fasting and your prayer."

4. Do many people go to hell today?

Most of them go to purgatory. Very few of them go directly to heaven. The Blessed Virgin said to the four visionaries who saw hell: "Here is the punishment for those who do not love God. Many people go there".

5. Should we act according to our own perception of priests?

Many people today depend upon the priest's faith. If priests are not good, that means that God does not exist. The Virgin Mary said: "Do not go to church to look at the priests and their private lives, but to pray and to listen to the word of God given by the priests".

6. How does the devil act today?

The devil infiltrates couples. He does not possess them; but his influence is such that there are many divorces. The Blessed Virgin says that *family prayer* is the only way to keep the devil away. We should have at least one blessed article in the house (e.g., a crucifix) and also the house should be blessed regularly.

The devil also infiltrates monasteries. He seeks to turn true believers into nonbelievers. Prayer, renunciation and charity become unimportant... One begins to live only on a human level, forgetting the spiritual and supernatural dimension: prayer, fasting and penance.

7. How does the Virgin Mary stress the importance of faith and its expression?

The Blessed Virgin told Mirjana that everyone must be converted before it is too late and must never put aside God and faith. "Let everything go but this." How many Christians are contenting themselves with praying occasionally to a far-off God! They have abandoned everything: Mass, Communion, the Sacrament of Reconciliation, prayer and fasting. They no longer live for God, Christ and the Church. Do they know that they are heading for damnation? Do they know that they should not laugh at God, and that Christ willed the establishment of the Church? Perhaps the Blessed Virgin is coming for the last time to show us the way to salvation.

8. What does the Blessed Virgin say about different religions?

One day, She told the visionaries: "In God, there are no divisions nor religions; divisions have been created by you in your world. The sole mediator is Jesus Christ. However, the fact that you belong to such or such a religion is not without importance." "The Spirit is not the same in all the churches."

9. Should we pray to Jesus or Mary?

At the request of a priest, the visionaries asked whether one should pray to Jesus or to Mary. She answered: "Pray to Jesus. I am His Mother and I intercede with Him for you. But, all prayers go to Jesus. I will help, I will pray, but everything does not depend on me; part of it depends on your own strength, on the strength of those who pray. As for your requests, come to me; I know the will of God better than you do".

27

10. *Is Mass important?*

"The Mass is the greatest prayer. You must prepare yourself for it, and must celebrate it with a pure and humble heart." In Medjugorje, the three to four hours of daily prayer always includes Mass.

11. *Is there a relationship between the apparitions of Fatima and those of Medjugorje?*

The similarity is striking. Fatima's message is an urgent call to repentance, prayer and penance. All this, in order to avoid war and to have peace on earth. Mary then said that unless a sufficient number of people converted and repented, a more dreadful war was to follow that one. Indeed, a worse war broke out under Pope Pius XI. We know that Russia will spread its errors in the world, by instigating wars and persecutions in the Church. Pope John Paul II said about Fatima: "This message is one of repentance, along with an invitation to prayer and to the Rosary. It is a warning".

In Medjugorje, the Blessed Virgin invites us to conversion, prayer, fasting, saying the Rosary and to the Sacrament of Reconciliation; and the warning is clear.

12. *How should we reply to the often-mentioned objection concerning the duration and the frequency of the apparitions?*

The visionaries are trained and taught individually by the Virgin Mary. Like a good teacher, She takes her time. On the other hand we must not forget that the visionaries have been chosen to live and transmit a message; the Blessed Virgin is preparing them for this task. As mentioned by Father Faricy, S.J., there is also an œcumenical aspect. Within the villages which form the parish of Medjugorje, there are Moslem, Orthodox and Catholic regions. Now, the Blessed Virgin is coming for the whole world.

13. *Does the Blessed Virgin speak about catastrophes?*

Yes, since a part of the message includes 10 secrets referring to some impending catastrophes and the way to mitigate them. To do this, we must be totally converted by faith, daily prayer, the monthly Sacrament of Reconciliation, fasting and the Rosary (15 decades).

14. *What about the prophetic vision of Pope Leo XIII?*

According to the information available, Pope Leo XIII had, on October 13, 1884, an ecstasy which lasted ten minutes. His face was flooded with light. He heard two voices: one was gentle, and the other was harsh. These were the voices of God and Satan. Satan asked God to give him free rein in his Church for a period of 100 years, so that he could destroy it. God accepted. Pope Leo XIII then composed a prayer to St. Michael the Archangel to be said at the end of Mass.

Now, that century ended on October 13, 1984. On that day, two hundred priests were in Medjugorje, and witnessed the apparition of the Blessed Virgin to the visionaries.

15. *Who can attest that these apparitions are true?*

The Church will have sooner or later the responsibility of approving the apparitions reported in the small village of Medjugorje in Yugoslavia. However, one can conclude that they are true by looking at the results. These young people are too humble and truthful to be putting on an act. The doctrine is solid and beyond their understanding. The devil would never want us to be converted by faith, prayer, the Rosary, fasting and the Sacrament of Reconciliation. The results of the apparitions in the life of the parish and the pilgrims are so positive, that they are a strong proof that this comes from Mary. *However, it is up to the spiritual authorities to make a final judgment.*

Conclusion

We wanted to prepare a relatively short text to tell people what is happening in Medjugorje. These apparitions of the Blessed Virgin are calling out to us and inviting the whole world to conversion.

To those who have read this text: please tell all your relatives and close friends about the Blessed Virgin's requests. Find out more about what is being lived in Medjugorje by reading more detailed literature. The Blessed Virgin is appearing in this village to bring us a message of peace and salvation. During the ten days we spent in Medjugorje, we assisted at seven apparitions and prayed with the youngsters every night. The undefinable scent of roses rising from the visionaries after the apparitions was for us the sign that we had asked from our heavenly Mother. Yes, Mary, blessed among all women, pray for us now and at the hour of our death.

Part Two

Interview

October 17, 1984

Father Tomislav Vlasić, O.F.M. (T.V.)
Spiritual director of the visionaries

and

Father Massimo Rastelli, S.J. (M.R.)
Father Guy Girard, S.SS.A. (G.G.)

M.R. — *Father Vlasić, we know how the apparitions began. It is now October 1984. Can you comment on the last messages?*

T.V. — There is something new in two ways: first of all, in what the Blessed Virgin does, secondly, in what the Blessed Virgin says.

What She does: I can say that She is attracting more and more people; even in the fall, which is the quiet season, the church is always full. Visitors come from all over Europe, the United States and Canada. Lately, there have been many priests in Medjugorje. On Saturday, October 13, 1984, two hundred priests were present, and one hundred and fifty two of them concelebrated the Mass. They came in a pilgrimage composed of priests and other pilgrims. We perceive that the Blessed Virgin is attracting more and more people, and whoever comes once wants to come back again.

What She says: The Blessed Virgin continues to invite us to prayer, fasting and conversion. The intervention of the Blessed Virgin to attract a crowd is something sympathetic, simple and very deep for me. Here is the latest message given to the parishioners (you must remember that it has been raining for three weeks; the vines have been almost totally destroyed):

> *"In the midst of your hardship, continue to offer your fatigue, and everything you have to God, and do not worry; God sends you these hardships because he loves you".*

In this message, we can see that the Blessed Virgin is looking after all the little details, even the material ones, and that God is present everywhere, and is taking care of everything. The last messages show us that He is with his people in all the events of their lives.

M.R. — *How do the local people accept these messages?*

T.V. — They accept these messages; however, everybody, including all the pilgrims must try to understand the apparitions of Medjugorje. There is one feature which differentiates these apparitions from those of Lourdes and Fatima: in the latter cases, the apparitions lasted only a few weeks or a few months. Those of Medjugorje began on June 24, 1981, and are still going on. We asked why so long and so often. The visionaries answer that the Blessed Virgin said that these apparitions are the last on earth. However, they refuse to explain the meaning of the word "last" for they claim that by doing so, they would have to reveal the secret. Beyond these things, we should see that the Blessed Virgin is guiding the people of Medjugorje. Indeed, She gives messages concerning *each step along the way*. Therefore, if we want to understand the messages, we must consider the context. For example, during a crisis that I do not want to describe, I asked the following question to the Blessed Virgin through one of the visionaries: "What should I do now?" To this, she answered me with a deep peace:

"Pray, fast, and let God act! You cannot imagine how powerful God is!"

As you can see, in response to a given question, comes a very simple answer which shines in our hearts. So throughout the "progress" of these persons, the pilgrims and all those who are following these messages, these answers come for their spiritual growth. That is why we must consider this aspect while keeping the future in mind. Those who want to apply Medjugorje's messages in their lives must progress in their spiritual lives. The Blessed Virgin wants the whole world to go further, so that it may deepen and live its faith. We must not consider these messages to be an end in themselves, but we must discover their depth. This is the only way to accept them.

Those who want to understand the messages must persevere in order to reach union with God. I think at this moment of all the world leaders who must join those who have experienced a rebirth of faith because of these events. They too must thoroughly examine these messages and apply them in their lives so that they can lead the people. The Blessed Virgin gave the following message to the priests:

"My very dear sons, today my son Jesus has allowed me to gather you here in order to give this message to you and to all those who love me. My very dear sons, pray constantly! Ask the Holy Spirit to inspire you always. In all your requests and in all your actions desire nothing but to carry out essentially the holy will of God. My very dear sons, thank you for having answered my call to come here!"

From a national point of view, this message has no meaning; however, for those with an open heart, it can make them look deeper into their faith, and help them make progress. This message is a call to deepen our faith every day.

Another aspect of the message refers to those who are watching from a distance and waiting for the approval of the Church authorities in this matter. To them, the Blessed Virgin says:

"One must of course follow the authority of the Church, but in the meantime, while awaiting the Church's decision,

one must make spiritual progress. The Church cannot make a judgment in a vacuum but only in a confirmation which presupposes a growth up belief in the child. First of all, must come birth, *followed by* baptism, *and then* confirmation. *The Church will confirm what is born from God. We must continue to progress in spiritual life as we are shaken up by these messages".*

G.G. — *I noticed that the Blessed Virgin underlines what we generally take for granted. It concerns very simple matters which become more difficult in practice, doesn't it?*

T.V. — Of course, but if we examine the History of the Church, as well as the History of Salvation, we will see that the problem is that we have been too superficial. This is not because we did not have the means to go deeply into our faith or because during that period of the History of the Church, we had extraordinary means, *but simply because some people and some communities did not go deep enough.* In this respect, I am thinking of an experience that I had a few weeks ago. I went to a chapel of nuns where they showed me a new crucifix and asked me my opinion of it. I answered that it was only a projection. Indeed, I saw a Christ who was neither standing nor hanging. I did not see him crying or suffering; I saw him as a superficial thing, not like *someone who was pierced and suffering,* but like a modern man who does not cry and whose faith is not deep enough. If we want these messages to bring salvation as does the Gospel, we must suffer and cry, suffer deeply.

M.R. — *Another impression that I have is that the Blessed Virgin is always asking for more and more. She is asking more and more for what you previously called "progress". However, I feel that people have a particular way of responding, and more importantly they feel the power of God. The more they endeavor to make some sacrifices, the more they receive. For example, we are under the impression that it is difficult to fast; however, once we begin to do so, it becomes enjoyable, easy, etc.*

T.V. — I have two comments to make in this regard: when the Blessed Virgin gives us new obligations, She intends to urge us to go more deeply into our faith. And another thing: on August 5, 1984, I asked the people to say part of their Rosary for the success of the International Eucharistic Congress. I asked the people if they were ready to say a part of the Rosary each day. They answered: "YES", but once they had left they had second thoughts. They were scared that they would not have time to do it. One month later, a gentleman said: "Now I can say 5 Rosaries a day". When people get involved, they find out that they always have more and more time, and when they love, there is always room for more love. Little by little, as you search for God, your capacity increases and as the Gospel says: "To everyone who has, even more will be given" (Luke 19:26).

G.G. — *I also noticed that those who say "We are told that the Blessed Virgin is appearing" do not seem to produce anything. Whereas, those who say "Mary is in Medjugorje" are experiencing a new power. The main message is that Mary is here. She is everywhere, but She appears here, and grace is related to this. What do you think of this?*

T.V. — This is a mystery, but I can tell you that the Blessed Virgin is wherever we find an open heart. However, grace is particularly noticeable at Medjugorje. One of the last messages given to the parishioners of Medjugorje at the end of September reads as follows:

"Be thankful to God who has allowed me to be among you for such a long time. It is a special gift!"

That's the way it is! There are some people who accept and others who don't. We must journey with those who believe and those who don't. As a priest, I must journey with everyone to be faithful to the spirit of my order and its roots. Just like St. Francis and St. Ignatius did. They grew through prayer, fasting, etc. An order cannot renew itself without going back to its roots. St. Ignatius practiced prayer. Everyone, whether they believe or not, can call upon the heart of the Church which is the core of holiness, and make progress together. In this way, they will discover the Blessed Virgin's grace and will receive her help. Many priests know these things, but are often unable to put them into practice. It is easy to talk about penance, but it is difficult to practice it. In my community, my brethren respect my decision to fast, but they do not go along with me on it.

G.G. — *We are now rediscovering the merits of deep prayer and fasting. We, the priests, have introduced in the pulpit many elements of psychology, of sociology, of science to explain things in scientific jargon.*

T.V. — When one visionary was asked: "Have you grown in faith?". She answered: "Yes". But to the question "Have you grown in the knowledge of God through the catechism?", She answered: "No". The words are deep, but theoretical. I myself have given science to people instead of giving them God. God gives through prayer and penance, but it is difficult to get involved in this way *if the merits of fasting are not recognized.* People are afraid to become weak, they must work, etc. We must point out that there are two forces in the individual with which we are dealing: *an aggressive force* through which the individual fights and needs to eat and assert himself on the human level. However, as stated by St. Paul, there exists another *force: the interior one.* We must discover this force, which comes from God, through fasting. When I give up everything to rely on God, His strength gives me strength.

M.R. — *Some people claim that pilgrimages are not important; we can pray at home.*

T.V. — It is as if you were saying to people not to go out for walks; these people would never discover new horizons — this is purely on the human level.

On the spiritual level, it is the same thing. At these places of pilgrimage, people receive a special strength, as well as particular graces. (We should go more than once a year.) I personally think that it is about time that we revitalize all the shrines dedicated to Mary in order to strengthen the faith. Each shrine must be like an oasis on the journey, a refuge to show the way, and help the people of God to make progress. Lourdes, Fatima, Guadalupe, Medjugorje will be real shrines if they foster the development of *spiritual dynamism.* Only with this interior life can we remain faithful to the Blessed Virgin. When the Angel asked Mary if She wanted to become the Mother of God, Mary prayed, then accepted. She raised the Child, etc. We must do the same if we want to be like Mary. Immobility kills, but movement gives life. Priests must give people the hope of salvation which Mary brought.

M.R. — *This pilgrim people is the parish. You have said previously that the Blessed Virgin is speaking to all the members of the parish; can you explain this statement?*

T.V. — The Blessed Virgin is speaking to the whole parish and *to all those who want to follow her.* She speaks to the parish because the latter takes up one's whole life. Indeed, those who join a parish receive graces, which they cannot even understand. Thus, it is important that the parish fulfill this role. The ideal for the parish should be to live the Blessed Virgin's messages. This will allow those who come to the parish to receive this strength.

M.R. — *The people who arrived yesterday said that they were impressed by the intensity of the prayer, free of all distractions — even the youngsters began to pray.*

T.V. — As priests, we must understand one thing: often, we discuss and preach in a scientific way, and people do not understand what we are saying. If we pray, people will follow us: we should practice what we preach; we should give an example of the interior life. If we live our Christianity, without bothering about what others say, then, they will feel the strength of our message.

M.R. — *One more thing. A few months ago, you were telling us, among the messages,* how sensitive the Blessed Virgin is to the Mass.

I remember one sentence: "Whenever you go to Mass, you should not receive communion without preparing for it and taking the time for thanksgiving."

T.V. — There are some simple and profound messages about the Mass. For example: One of the visionaries once said that the Blessed Virgin was crying and She said:

"You come to church and you go back home without knowing what you've learned. I do not want to guide you this way!"

Once She said:

"If you want to live your Mass, start praying as soon as you leave for church; each time you come to church, you should be in a meditative mood; never go to Mass without a pure heart and never leave the church without thanksgiving."

This teaches us a lesson. These are small details, but we always seem to be in a rush. On July 16, 1984, the Blessed Virgin told Jelena that She would no longer appear to her for a certain period of time, in order to test her. The young girl prayed and the Blessed Virgin reappeared to her saying:

"Congratulations! You did not let Satan influence you; the Mass that you attended tonight is important because you attended it with devout silence, you received a gift. So, I appeared to you sooner."

The real strength of the Mass comes when we live it with our heart! God wants to save the world and whoever wants to follow Him is able to do so, even if he has to undergo some hardships because it is God who has decided to bring us salvation.

M.R. — *How did you accept your transfer to another place (Vitina); once you had left Medjugorje, how close were you to God?*

T.V. — You must understand that the Blessed Virgin does not appear to someone for himself, but to bring him closer to God; so I can be very close to God here. My attitude must be to worship God, and to abandon myself to Him in all circumstances, for He is my guide. Even in difficult times, it is God who directs everything; we only have *to place ourselves in His hands.*

M.R. — *I think that since you are here, you will preach during Mass the same way as you did in Medjugorje, since you cannot* *separate your experience and your life. I think that the people will listen to you and will come in great numbers, attracted by the Blessed Virgin's message, as it concerns Neapolitan people who usually respond very well to messages from heaven.*

T.V. — That's true! We are mistaken when we think that people are only attracted by material things, leisure and amusements. They are hungry for God. In church, we should not talk about God the same way we do in school. If people can see in us the example of a real Christian life, then, they will follow us. To live a life of prayer, we don't have to be philosophers. We, priests, often talk about prayer in a theoretical way: we look for themes, etc., whereas it would suffice to simply live prayerfully: to get down on our knees, take up our Rosary, think and desire to pray. The breviary, the Rosary, the Gospel, the sacraments should be sufficient for us.

M.R. — *What other messages has the Blessed Virgin given to the parish this month, October 1984, besides those that you have already explained?*

T.V. — Each time, the Blessed Virgin said:

"My dear children..."

The visionaries told me to repeat to the people: "The Blessed Virgin says to you:

"My dear children"

May the people allow themselves to be kissed by the Blessed Virgin who is saying:

"My dear children"

The Blessed Virgin follows everyone of us calling him:

"My dear son"

even the weak, the sick... The Blessed Virgin kisses each one saying:

"My dear child".

Let this message be enough for your life!

M.R. — *You said that many people are hungering for God, and it is true. However, we can see that many people are turning to oriental religions, and are following the gurus, who are people who live what they preach.*

T.V. — Curiosity plays a part! Furthermore, we often have presented Jesus on a theoretical level rather than showing an authentic practice of the faith, and we have been unable to lead our youth into the depths of spiritual life. In recent years, theology has become too rational; thus it cannot guide people to a deep spiritual life. We have lost the mystique of the Middle Ages. Rahner said: "In the 1980's, the Christians who believe in Jesus will be the Christian mystics". When we seek Jesus with conviction and sincerity, we will no longer feel the need to turn to the oriental gurus.

M.R. — *There is a difference between these oriental cultures which fascinate Christians.*

T.V. — The difference is a religious one. Christianity was revealed to us by Jesus Christ and in the fullness of the Revelation of Jesus Christ. Buddhism gives us human and religious wisdom, but it does not have Revelation.

In God, we do not meet a philosopher, an absolute being, etc., but rather a God who is Father, Mother, Brother. So we are intimate with God and the things of the hereafter are not unknown to us. That is why it is easier to make progress in spiritual life. Revelation makes it easier to come close to God.

G.G. — *In one message, Our Lady said:*

"Tell all my children that their conversion must not be delayed".

Can you explain why the message of the Blessed Virgin is so urgent?

T.V. — There are some people who think immediately about the end of the world. I believe that there is an urgent need for conversion of heart. Some people are far from God, so they must be saved by me, by you, by all of us. The Church reaches full enlightenment faster, and she must enlighten the others. The Blessed Virgin says that the secrets are conditional. If we live these messages with all our soul, others will be enlightened and led to salvation.

M.R. — *At this time, we often hear about apparitions, which are sacred manifestations related to Mary and to God. These are almost a violation of the order of things (the expression may be too strong) which tinges the Medjugorje event with a Marian image of a Virgin who is crying, whose face is covered with tears.*

T.V. — I cannot talk about the practical details of the apparitions, because I do not know the particular facts; however, I do know that any graces which lead us close to God should be welcomed. The Church has the responsibility to ascertain the facts and verify their authenticity. *But I think we are making a mistake if we wait for the Church's final decision before forming an opinion.* So, in all these events, we should accept whatever is positive, whatever leads us to God, and reject whatever is negative. In one message, Our Lady said to Jelena (when we asked a question about the discernment of spirits):

"Everything which leads us to God is a gift of God, for Satan is essentially a negative being, and leads you to the negative".

We, priests, must accept and treasure the graces which lead us to God, and eliminate the human element, i.e. everything which could be generated by our own psyche. We know that some Saints suffered from nervous disorders, but they became holy because they accepted God's grace.

M.R. — *We, Italians, are pessimistic about young people who take the wrong road; yet, I work in a college where I also see students who are a source of hope for me. I also know many organizations which are very good and very popular. Why this pessimism, even among religious who, because of their work, do not even realize the riches they hold right in their own hands? Can you give us a few words of hope about our Italian youth?*

T.V. — I am very optimistic about young people, but we must remember that Jesus has sent us to preach the Gospel, not in a theoretical way. He has given us the power of the Holy Spirit. With Him, we are stronger than evil (drugs, sex, etc.). Let's go forward with courage without pretending to be able to change a Parish or the world with the first sermon. Let us begin, in practice, with the grandmothers of our Parish, and we will eventually reach the children, the youth also. We must embark on the road of prayer and fasting to challenge the world. Then, we will find ways to improve the world.

M.R. — *Father, could you tell me what message the Blessed Virgin would give to my young people today? When I go back to my community, and with my students, what could I tell them?*

T.V. — When you go to these young people, always go with Our Lady, and in Her Name, never alone.

The apparitions are a special grace; we will never thank Heaven enough for this Gift. Death and resurrection are the roots of all spirituality. When we tell people this, we revive their faith and they ask us what to do... We must tell these people what the Gospel says. We must tell them: "Live the Mass, be charitable to your neighbour!" The role of the Blessed Virgin is the role of a mother who wakes us up and who invites us to pray, and to act with faith. Therefore, act in such a way that your young people will be touched and that their faith and love will be awakened.

M.R. — *One question about the visionaries: we hear that Jelena* has an inner illumination and sees the Blessed Virgin. Marijana sees Her in church, during Mass.*

T.V. — We must not pay too much attention to details. Both of them see the Blessed Virgin every day; they hear Her voice. Jelena has a more developed gift, a deeper way. Anyway, it is the kind of gift which leads to mystical experiences.

M.R. — *There is one problem in accepting the messages: we see some contradictions, and we know that Our Lady cannot contradict herself.*

---

* Jelena Vasily and Marijana Vasily have been granted the gift of a charism. They do not see the Blessed Virgin, but perceive Her in their hearts.

T.V. — As far as I am concerned and as far as I can see there are no contradictions. These can come from within the person who is speaking, some words forgotten through tiredness, or to wish to stress one part of the message more than another. We can also find this type of contradiction in the Bible. We must be objective and look for the essential part of Our Lady's message which is transmitted by the visionaries who, in this respect, fully agree, and are one hundred percent sure.

G.G. — *One last thought about the relationship between prayer and fasting. The fact that the Blessed Virgin insists on fasting shocks people a little and especially priests. (One of them told me that fasting is an end not a starting point.) Could you elaborate a little on this means which leads us more quickly to God?*

T.V. — I think that both, prayer and fasting, go together. One cannot fast without praying deeply and one cannot pray without fasting.

We are talking about the same thing: when I fast, I am giving up something for God (hunger does not interest me), because I am seeking God. I renounce life's pleasures; I am happy even in suffering, because I am seeking God. Prayer is seeking God, so praying and fasting are the same thing.

I do not agree with the priest who says that fasting is an end. On the contrary, if I want to come closer to God, I must begin by giving up something. In a broad sense, fasting is giving up evil and everything which leads me away from God.

Part Three

Testimony

Ten days in Medjugorje
October 11 to 21, 1984

Father Guy Girard, S.SS.A.

It is with great joy that I write these lines to testify to the ten grace-filled days we spent in Medjugorje.

The priests's retreat in Rome was over. Six thousand priests and more than a hundred bishops had taken part in it. The Holy Father had celebrated the Eucharist with these priests who came from different countries. This celebration was wonderful and the Pope cried with joy when presented with a book bearing the signature of each priest along with the name of the country he was from. I felt a great joy in my heart and in my soul but I remained dissatisfied. I still felt a longing, a thirst. There was another source from which I must drink. I had come as a pilgrim to Rome and prayed a lot. I had experienced the universality of the Church with my brother priests.

Leaving the magnificent basilica of St. Peter along with eight other Canadian priests we were to find ourselves in another basilica, one not built by men but by the Virgin Mary, in the small village of Medjugorje, in Yugoslavia. The Blessed Virgin had been appearing there every day since June 24, 1981. I had been reading about this and friends had been talking about it. In all simplicity, I had asked the Blessed Virgin to plan this trip for my brother, Father Armand, and myself, if such was the will of our Eternal Father. Mary heard my prayer; She planned everything. Mysteriously guided by Her during those ten days, I went through an incredible spiritual experience. In all my life there has never been anything like it. Since my reception of the sacraments and the priesthood, this is where God's grace has been most abundant.

Beginning on the first day we prayed in the church of Medjugorje, which seems to have sprung up out of the earth in this small plain surrounded by mountains. We prayed there with hundreds of pilgrims who had arrived from everywhere very early in the afternoon. We said the Rosary at 5 o'clock, then we said it again, and then at about 5:45 the pastor of the parish, Father Barbarić, invited the priests to join the pilgrims who were already in the chapel of the apparitions.

A few moments later, the visionaries arrived; they stood facing the altar and started their prayer with the sign of the cross. But, what a sign of the cross! A sign of the cross filled with the TRINITY. When the Blessed Virgin appeared, the visionaries fell to their knees simultaneously, their eyes fixed on Her. The beauty and serenity of their faces reflected their happiness. But these human words cannot describe their ecstasy; it cannot be described, it must be seen, and we saw this ecstasy of the visionaries...!

Mass was celebrated and the immense crowd of pilgrims shared *as never before,* in the greatness of this mystery. In a meditative and respectful mood, we participated in the sacrifice of Jesus who offers himself to the Father for the salvation of the world. Only Mary could prepare hearts and souls for this most sublime action. This was the first day: a sort of "creation". It was beyond our understanding, especially if this were not the work of God.

Then there was the second day. Providentially, we eight Canadian priests met Marija, one of the visionaries. She simply invited us to her home. In the small living room her mother served us coffee. We chatted a little, within the limitations imposed by the language barrier, despite an interpreter's help. Then we prayed together to the Blessed Virgin. She united our hearts in a common prayer. We asked the Blessed Virgin to give us a message through Marija during the apparition of October 13, our third day in Medjugorje.

The church was full as it is every day. We were two hundred priests and we could not fit into the chapel of the apparitions. The pastor of the parish invited all the priests to go to the basement of the rectory. The young visionaries came there to pray to the Blessed Virgin. She appeared to them for a longer time. The visionaries radiated a real beauty; each one according to his age and personality. The Blessed Virgin had a message for Her priests.[1]

On the morning of October 14, we were already leaving Medjugorje by car for Split, to board the ship and cross over to Italy. During the car ride, I felt, deep in my heart, a pressing invitation to stay a week longer. Why? I don't know. But the further we got from Medjugorje, the more pressing was the call. It was like an incessant wave striking me and calling me. I really didn't know the reason for that call which mingled with the HAIL MARYS that I was reciting. But I felt more and more certain. It was not an obligation, nor even a need. It was a call from the Blessed Virgin. I knew it! Without understanding why, I was sure of it!

It was only when I got out of the car that I shared these things with my twin brother, a priest himself. He had felt the same thing. I had asked the Blessed Virgin for this sign, in order to be sure that it wasn't an illusion.

So, after leaving our traveling companions, we returned to Medjugorje. This didn't seem to surprise them. On the contrary, they encouraged us to return and draw more from the source, so that we could then share with them the experience we were about to live.

It was with joy that we reentered that small village which had now become a *holy land* to us. We recognized faces marked by the sun and hard work. These women who work so hard and these men who cultivate vines and tobacco had now become our brothers and sisters. They would continually greet us and offer

---

1. This message may be found on page 17.

us grapes. They didn't understand our language nor did we understand theirs, but their warmth and their smiles spoke to us of the Love of God and neighbor.

I still remember that old lady who was walking towards the mountain of the cross and who offered her walking stick to a deacon; not a word, but what a loving gesture! I no longer had any doubts that the Blessed Virgin was coming regularly here to Medjugorje. All these people revealed, by their lives deeply rooted in prayer, the face of Jesus himself.

Mary had molded their faces into the image of Her Son. *Everybody,* men, women, teenagers and children *pray* three hours a day and seven days a week. It is hard not to believe that all this comes from God. The fire, started by the Blessed Virgin Mary in that Yugoslavian country, can never be put out. Let those who do not believe go there with a walking stick in hand, as if going to the PROMISED LAND, but not with a camera to look for the marvelous or the extraordinary.

I will never forget the night we prayed on the hill of the apparitions.

Marija, one of the visionaries, always welcomed us. My brother and I were now part of the family. We shared the bread her mother baked. From that wonderful home, whose backyard faces the hill of the apparitions, we climbed up the path to join the visionaries and a few other young people. There, hidden behind a few bushes, unnoticed by occasional visitors, we prayed to the Blessed Virgin and we sang together until midnight. The singing and the PRAYERS were not lost in the night which was already quite cold. They drifted up to the heart of the Blessed Virgin like a precious fragrance that the Servant of God was offering to the Blessed Trinity.

There was nothing deceitful about these young people. They knew two priests were there with them. They knew how much we loved them. The affection we had for those young people was not primarily because the Blessed Virgin was appearing to them but because they were people of prayer.

Nor will we ever forget another night, when we climbed the mountain of the cross. Secretly, a word had been passed around to organize a little group which we joined. Once again, the night was cold; we walked, reciting the Rosary. We discreetely lit the path with a small lamp, and once at the top, after an hour's walking, the forty or so of us knelt for a long time in silence. Then, standing up, we got together to sing hymns to Mary or to say the Rosary. We were united with heaven. Nothing artificial, nothing prepared in advance, nothing programmed. Our hearts just opened spontaneously to pray under the inspiration of the Holy Spirit. Then, we climbed down the mountain and the group broke up to go and say the Rosary in their homes. Pilgrims and priests were always numerous. For three or four hours a day, a fervent prayer rose up to Heaven. Large numbers of pilgrims longing for absolution and pardon would go to be absolved.

In that church no one is influenced by anyone else. People come to pray. Lives are transformed. People turn back to God. Faith, *grown cold,* is rekindled. We can never go back to what we were. The hearts of thousands of pilgrims are set on fire. The Christian community of Medjugorje unites their prayers with those of the visionaries who don't consider themselves, in any way, superior to anyone else. There are as well those days of fasting on bread and water to help us remain faithful to our own conversion and to pray for the conversion of the world.

Yes, I cannot believe that such excellent fruits are not from God. Personally, I am convinced that Mary is coming once again to give an urgent message to mankind. Mary continually reminds us of the Gospel's insistence on constant prayer, conversion, faith, and fasting. Certainly, someday the Church will rule on the authenticity of the apparitions, *but we should not wait to change our lives.*

If I truly believe that I have seen in 1984 a living community similar to that of the early Church, and if I believe that the spiritual experience being lived there can only be divine, then I have no right to be silent.

Conclusion

1. Those ten days in Medjugorje allowed me to meet most of the visionaries. My contact with them convinced me that they are perfectly normal and well balanced.

2. The parishioners are people of prayer with a remarkable, dynamic faith. They challenge us by their lives of prayer, fasting and charity.

3. The priests and nuns are witnesses of God. Their fervent sermons are nourished by prayer. They are not looking for glory but try to answer the needs of the parishioners and pilgrims with a tireless patience.

4. The numerous conversions are already a remarkable sign that the Virgin Mary's call has been heard.

5. What the Blessed Virgin is asking for: PEACE, FAITH, DAILY PRAYER (Rosary), PENANCE (especially fasting), HOLY COMMUNION and the SACRAMENT OF RECONCILIATION; all these are already demanded by the Gospel. The Virgin Mary is putting us back into the heart of Jesus's message.

I am writing this testimony to thank the Blessed Virgin Mary for all she is doing for us. And also to assure the priests, the men and women religious, as well as the parishioners of Medjugorje of my prayers so that they may be faithful witnesses of all that the Blessed Virgin is asking.

Father Guy Girard, S.SS.A.

Testimony

Ten days in Medjugorje
October 11 to 21, 1984

Father Armand Girard, S.SS.A.

It was in 1982 that I heard for the first time about the apparitions of the Blessed Virgin in Medjugorje. I didn't pay much attention, and it didn't interest me at the time. We often hear about apparitions of the Blessed Virgin, but without foundation. It seemed like just one more...

Months passed and a book came out by Father Laurentin concerning the apparitions in Medjugorje. Since this priest had been my teacher in Mariology during my studies in Theology, I immediately bought his book which was selling out quickly. Knowing Father Laurentin's objectivity, his sincerity, and his keen interest in Mariology, I read his book, and in my heart a dream took shape of going myself to see what was happening in this parish, lost in the mountains of Yugoslavia. I say dream because I didn't think that I would ever be able to go there.

At about that same time, I heard about a worldwide retreat for priests in Rome. This retreat would bring together close to six thousand priests from all over the world. It was by prolonging this retreat in Rome that I was able to get to Yugoslavia. However, I must say that even when I was already in Rome, I still doubted that I would go on a pilgrimage to Medjugorje. Could I get into that country, even with a visa? The Slavic language seemed to be a great handicap, and without a guide, what could we really do there? It was with great misgivings that I left Rome for that unknown country that disturbed me.

This testimony is that of a priest who was going to Medjugorje for three days and ended up staying there for *ten days...*

Life in Medjugorje

In Medjugorje, I lived within the Christian community the Gospel values found in the Acts of the Apostles. At the age of 48, after twenty years of priesthood, I dare say: "They were the ten best days of my life, and the best priest's retreat since my ordination". My retreat in Rome had left me a little dissatisfied; the Blessed Virgin was to complete my retreat here by the atmosphere of prayer that my soul longed for.

What surprised me most, was not first and foremost the visionaries, although I had been welcomed by them, but rather it was those poor people who came each day to pray for more than three hours in the church. Those humble people were eating up God's word like fresh bread. Their hearts seem to be centered on Holy Communion. They fast on bread and water twice a week to change their own lives and to serve, without knowing it, as a challenge for the whole world.

Never, in my whole life as a priest, have I ever seen such great charity. "See the great love they have for one another" (John 13:35). This example of their lives has brought me closer to the Heart of God and the Heart of Mary. When I was with these humble people, who have no pretentions, I felt that here prayer had become the very air that the parish breathes. And their prayer does not stop with the three hours spent in church, but it seems to rise up to God day and night. *Here, we don't talk about prayer, we pray.*

In this corner of the world, something is happening that is beyond reason. The love in the people's hearts *is "drinking up God"* like a glass of good cold water. Never, absolutely never, have I seen such faith. I also have a strong conviction that the hearts of those Christians are "welded" to the hearts of Jesus and Mary. The first Christians lived this way. "Each considered the other to be better than himself."

We are immersed in a sea of prayer! How refreshing it is for our parched souls which are dried up like sponges without water! Many people write about Medjugorje; they would do better to go over there instead!

The people of Medjugorje are ready to share everything with us. We don't speak their language, but it doesn't really matter. They speak the language of the heart and that language is universal. Yes, watching these people live, I understood that they are freer than we are. Our freedom is imprisoned in materialistic comfort, while they enjoy the freedom of the children of God, and *that freedom is within themselves.* No one can take it away from them; it is deep in their souls. Imprisoned, handcuffed, threatened, they are freer than we are. The TRUTH has set them free! The Gospel has set them FREE!

The values they hold are from the Gospel. We can do whatever we want against them, but we can't really hurt them. Those people are deeply rooted in the heart of God and in the heart of the Blessed Virgin Mary. For ten days, my brother, Father Guy and myself were *plunged* into the heart of that parish. We felt adopted by them, and it seemed as if we had known them all our life. Deep down, have we not the same MOTHER, THE BLESSED VIRGIN?

During those ten days, hundreds of priests and bishops passed through Medjugorje and we concelebrated together. Did some remain indifferent? If so, they were in the minority. I am certain that many priests go away transformed.

As for myself, I shall never be the same again. Something has changed inside of me, and that something smacks of eternity!

Meeting with the Visionaries

The Blessed Virgin Mary granted us many great favours during our stay in Medjugorje. We met the visionaries and their families. It is thanks to our little sister Marija that we met the other visionaries. It is such a great joy to meet those young people who love Mary so much and are so loved by Her. It was with Marija that we prayed the first time. We went with her to see Vicka and her parents, and on the way we met Ivan and his parents working in the tobacco fields. We ended our stroll at Jakov's house playing soccer. How refreshing! What a wonderful atmosphere! Two Canadian priests playing around kicking a bal¹ with Jakov, Marija and Vicka at the foot of the mountain of the Cross... And I also believe that the Blessed Virgin was spoiling us, Guy and myself. A spirit of connivance developed between the visionaries and ourselves. They told us about the places where they pray. At night, after Mass, we would go to Marija's. She would give us warmer clothes, since the nights are cold, and we would climb the hill of the apparitions, reciting the Rosary. Reaching the predetermined spot, we would meet other young people who belonged to the prayer group. We would spend a few hours reciting HAIL MARYS, singing the praises of the Blessed Virgin, and listening to the silence of the night. Then a little before midnight, we would go back to Marija's place.

Another night, we climbed the mountain of the Cross which is 540 m. high (1625 feet). Some older people belong to this other prayer group. We had to go a long way in the dark lit only by small pocket flashlights that we were advised to use sparingly. I recall the sight of these people at the top of the mountain. Everyone knelt down in front of the cross and kissed the ground before starting the Rosary and the singing. There, in the middle of the night, I thought about the whole world for whom we were about to pray, and I felt that a little bit of heaven was touching that holy place. We were the only two priests on that mountain. We did not know the people who had prayed with us during that long climb, but our prayer united us.

That narrow stony road reminded me of the road to perfection of Saint Teresa of Avila. These two prayer groups extend behond the group of the visionaries and I think that they are vitally necessary so that the flame of FAITH may *never* go out here.

These are special moments that unite us with the INVISIBLE.

In the silence of the night, those HAIL MARYS seemed to me to protect that village and that countryside against all the attacks of the evil one. After these prayers, we climbed down the mountain again still praying; then we broke up and went to pray somewhere else.

Guy and I returned to Marija's. In their small parlor, we gave thanks for the day which was now coming to an end. I believe that those who went to Medjugorje as tourists will never understand the joy of the pilgrim.

We shared the noon meal at Marija's and also spent many evenings together. Everything was always simple, warm and friendly.

The Chapel of the Apparitions

During my ten days in Medjugorje, I managed to be present at six of the apparitions of the Blessed Virgin Mary to the visionaries. This was a great privilege for me. We were between thirty and forty priests in that little chapel. For so many to get in, it was necessary to remain standing through the whole Rosary. We go in before the visionaries arrive and pray to the Virgin Mary. When the visionaries arrive, they take their place in front of the small altar and begin to pray.

With very great devotion, they begin with the sign of the cross. After a few moments of prayer, they kneel simultaneously, their eyes fixed on the Blessed Virgin Mary, whom they watch with indescribable joy. It is an ecstasy, that lasts from three to four minutes. No words or human speech can describe what happens here. We sense that these youngsters, very different one from the other, share the same joy. Nothing distracts them. The flash-bulbs of the cameras, the presence of the priests, the overpowering heat of that small chapel, nothing disturbs that ecstasy. They are beyond time, their eyes fixed on their Heavenly Mother. We cannot hear anything, but we can see that there is a dialogue going on between the Mother and her children. Then, it all ends with a barely audible single word, that I finally understood when I returned to Canada: "ODE!", which means "She is gone!".

The youngsters go out of the room to continue praying and to attend Mass. They have gone back to being like everybody else, without special treatment, without being in the spotlight.

They go back home with their friends. There is only one thing that could single them out, the "HAIL MARY" they recite, it comes right from the heart. It springs full-blown from deep within, the fruit of their intimate dialogue with their Heavenly Mother.

I watched them and photographed them not out of curiosity, because, inside, I begged the Blessed Virgin to forgive my audacity, but rather to get at the truth. I saw them six times and each time it was new, as if it were the first time. When I was facing the visionaries, something made me kneel down and, very often, I could smell a fragrance which I cannot describe, but which brought me great interior peace. Those few moments moved me to pray to the Blessed Virgin Mary while basking in the Motherly tenderness She has for each one of us. These are divine moments that change a person's life, and I shall never be able to forget them.

"HAPPY THOSE WHO HAVE NOT SEEN, AND STILL BELIEVE!"

Conclusion

It is difficult for me to draw any conclusions about that pilgrimage to Medjugorje, because that pilgrimage was so full of Grace that I feel I've really said nothing. I want to emphasize that my fears were dissipated by the constant presence of the Virgin Mary. This Mother that Jesus gave us from the Cross protected me in such an obvious way that in spite of all the things that happened, which could have been maddening or even serious, I never felt the slightest anxiety. Why be afraid? Our Mother was with us. Day after day, She showed me the way, guiding me with the delicate embrace of motherly love. It was probably the first time that my blind eyes were opened to the spiritual dimensions of the divine Maternity of Mary.

This pilgrimage helped me to understand that praying to the Blessed Virgin is not an extra devotion that we should have. Her presence in our priestly life is an absolute necessity. Mother of

Christ the priest, She is the very air that surrounds all our pastoral activities.

To conclude this testimony, I want to say to those who will read it: "The call of the Blessed Virgin is the call of the Gospel":

"PRAY, PRAY OFTEN"

"GO TO CONFESSION EVERY MONTH"

"FAST ON BREAD AND WATER, ESPECIALLY ON FRIDAYS"

"DO PENANCE"

"ABANDON YOURSELF TO THE FATHER'S WILL".

I dare hope that these few pages will help to fulfill the Virgin Mary's wishes at Medjugorje. It is in complete submission to the authority of the Church that I wrote this testimony. It was impossible for me not to say what this pilgrimage has meant to me personally.

United in prayer in Jesus and Mary,

Father Armand Girard, S.SS.A.

To the Reader

You who have read these lines, may you commit yourself to following the REQUESTS of Mary. Without any shadow of a doubt, your heart will be renewed. Do not be afraid of fasting, of the Sacrament of Reconciliation, prayer, the Rosary, Holy Communion! Do not let yourself be led to believe that the Blessed Virgin is asking too much. Just get started. Your joy will be so great that you will know that it is from the Blessed Virgin and that it can only lead to Jesus.

G.G.

February 1985

A further *proof* of the *love* our Blessed Mother has for her children. The Queen of Peace has confirmed to us the authenticity of her apparitions by *signs*. *These signs are concrete and frequent.* We thank Her wholeheartedly. Our priesthood obliges us to secrecy and to obedience to the Church.

In witness whereof we have signed

Father Guy Girard, S.SS.A.
Father Armand Girard, S.SS.A.

Introduction to the Testimony
of Georgette Faniel

The true author of this testimony is Georgette Faniel, a Canadian woman of Belgian extraction, born in 1915 in Montreal where she still resides.

The gratuitous choice of the Eternal Father rested upon her in her early childhood. Indeed, at the age of six, she hears the voice of Jesus. This voice resounds in the depth of her heart (inner locutions), but also in her ear (aural locutions). Little by little, this dialogue with Jesus will become clear. Then she will hear the voice of the Father, that of Jesus, of the Holy Spirit and of the Virgin Mary. This constant dialogue will be a normal fact and part of her life. The intimacy of the Divine Persons and of the Virgin Mary with regards to her will grow constantly.

She sleeps about one or two hours a night. The rest of the night becomes hours of prayer for the world, for the spiritual renewal of the Church, for the holiness of the men and women consecrated to God. She also prays to sustain Our Holy Father Pope John Paul II, to praise the Virgin Mary and to glorify the Eternal Father.

This long life of intimacy with God has always remained hidden. In her spiritual notes, she writes, one day, that the Eternal Father told her: "LIKE MY SON, YOU WILL HAVE A PUBLIC LIFE." At the time she did not understand the meaning of this nor how this was to come about.

After seventy-two (72) years of hidden life, the Eternal Father shows her how to come out of her anonymity. If she listened to herself, she would refuse to give up her hidden life. But the Eternal Father asks her to die to her own will and to accept only His own. He tells her: "ACCEPT WITH LOVE THAT THE TESTIMONY ON MEDJUGORJE BE PUBLISHED SO THAT THE APPARITIONS MAY BE MADE KNOWN."

It is in obedience to this God she loves so much that she lets us in on what is dearest to her: her intimacy with the Blessed Trinity and with the Virgin Mary. This intimacy was recorded in the form of a dialogue by Fathers Armand and Guy Girard.

We hope that this presentation of Georgette Faniel will allow the reader to understand better what follows.

The Origin of this Testimony

As this testimony is of prime importance, we shall try to describe the context in which it came to be. My brother Guy and myself had made a pilgrimage to Medjugorje in October 1984. This had been a marvellous spiritual experience for us.

The following year, at the same time, after having made a private (spiritual) retreat of seven days in Rome, we could not help but answer the call of the Virgin Mary and we returned to Medjugorje. As a result of this new experience, we felt renewed.

In October 1985, we had had a private conversation with a Franciscan about the visible and frequent signs that the Virgin Mary produces through the servant of the Eternal Father, Georgette Faniel in Montreal.

At Medjugorje, through the mediacy of the visionary Marija, we succeeded in asking the Virgin Mary if the testimony and the visible signs which we had with Georgette FANIEL to prove the authenticity of the apparitions of the Virgin Mary at Medjugorje should be sent to the Holy Father. The Virgin Mary answered us:

"Dear children, pray and in prayer, God will enlighten you on what you must do. You will feel it in your hearts."

This answer appeared extraordinary to us for it concealed its profound meaning from everyone except those to whom it was addressed.

We came back to Canada renewed and confident. We prayed and meditated on all that was going on between Georgette and us relative to Medjugorje. Had the time come to say more? On November 16, 1985, I went to celebrate Holy Mass in the sanctuary dedicated to the Eternal Father of His little servant's home, the one to whom the Lord had granted very great favors. I requested that she ask the following question to Jesus:

"Ask Jesus during the Holy Eucharist: Must we speak of what is going on in Canada and which directly concerns the apparitions of the Blessed Virgin at Medjugorje?"

After this request had been made to Georgette, I celebrated Holy Mass. During this time, Georgette prayed before the Precious Blood in profound respect, and then she said:

"Jesus, I ask You, through the intercession of MARY, QUEEN OF PEACE, give us an answer. I beg You, Jesus, give us an answer!" (Prayer of intense supplication.)

Tears of joy ran from her eyes: "We have an answer."

"Why would I have inspired you to offer your life to bear witness to the authenticity of the apparitions of the Blessed Virgin at Medjugorje?"

This answer was given with authority by the Eternal Father. As a servant of the Father and bride of Jesus, Georgette Faniel recognizes the voice of her Creator immediately and without any hesitation. I recalled at that moment that, during Holy Week in 1985, the little servant of the Eternal Father had offered her life as a witness to the authenticity of the apparitions of the Blessed Virgin at Medjugorje.

It was after this answer of the Eternal Father to his servant Georgette that my brother Guy and I wrote this testimony in favor of Medjugorje. This text was confidential and was not to be published in any form. In Croatia, we sent it to two priests. One of them had it translated into the Croatian language and with our permission gave it to a few persons to read. He wrote to us: "It seems to me that Georgette, this gem of the Father, should not remain hidden anymore; let Georgette herself take courage and question those from heaven who speak to her! Neither the Father (the Eternal Father), nor the Mother (Mary, Queen of Peace) will be annoyed if she asks this question."

Therefore, we had to ask the Eternal Father whether it was His Holy and Adorable Will that this testimony be made public. This was done. On May 9, 1986, I went to celebrate Holy Mass at Georgette's place. Before beginning the Eucharist, I explained to her the necessity of questioning her speakers from heaven to find out if the "TESTIMONY IN FAVOR OF MEDJUGORJE" was to be made public. It was after the celebration of the Eucharist that I questioned the little servant of the Father.

A.G. — *Did you ask the question to your speakers from heaven and what was your question?*

G.F. — Yes, I asked the following question to the Eternal Father: *Is it Your Will, Most Holy Father, that the testimony of my life and the testimony in favor of Medjugorje be made public by revealing my name?*

A.G. — *What answer did you receive?*

G.F. — The Eternal Father answered this: *Why would I have kept you in warm soil for years, hidden from view, if not so that you may produce much fruit?*

A.G. — *Did you ask any other questions?*

G.F. — No, but I put in an objection!

A.G. — *An objection?*

G.F. — I said: *"If the seed does not die in the soil, it cannot bear fruit?*

A.G. — *And the Eternal Father said?*

G.F. — The Eternal Father replied: *I agree, but I want you to die to your own will!*

A.G. — *Did the Eternal Father add anything else to this answer?*

G.F. — Yes, He added: *I have already told you: Like my beloved Son, you will have a public life.*

A.G. — *Did He say anything else?*

G.F. — Yes.

A.G. — *What did He say?*

G.F. — He told me this: *Through the total gift of your life, you are the treasure of the Church where the lowly, the poor, the sick, the Church, all of mankind will go to acquire riches in face of our espousals. You are the beloved daughter of the Virgin Mary, Queen of Peace, and you are the gem of the Holy Trinity. By accepting Our Will, you live with your beloved spouse the total gift of yourself as priest and victim, to glorify Me and to sustain the Holy Father, the consecrated souls and humanity. Accept with love that this testimony be published to make known the authenticity of the apparitions. Renounce your own will to accept only Our Holy and Adorable Will on you. This act of surrender is the sublime act of your life as spouse of Christ, as mother of your spiritual children, as handmaid of the Blessed Trinity and as confidante of the Virgin Mary, Queen of Peace.*
We thank you and keep this peace of heart, soul and mind. The most beautiful gift you can offer us is to surrender your will. You are living at this moment the beautiful prayer of the complete gift of yourself. Commend your will into my hands as my Son did on the cross through love. You must die as a victim of our love for the Church and for mankind which I have entrusted to you. Remain faithful to us to the end, then it will be the beginning of a new life with Us for eternity.

A.G. — *I thank you with all my heart for having given me this clear answer coming from the Eternal Father.*

G.F. — This was not easy for Satan was constantly trying to blur the voice of the Eternal Father, but the Queen of Peace was defending me.

A.G. — *Thank you very much.*

Inner and Aural Locutions

A.G. — *Given that, with the permission of the Eternal Father, we have decided to speak, in my opinion, the best thing would be that you tell the story of your life, of the divine action in you in the form of a dialogue. This would be simpler and give more credibility to your story. Do you agree?*

G.F. — If you wish but this will be very painful to me.

A.G. — *Georgette, I know that it is most painful for you to answer the questions of my brother Guy and myself, for you were telling me that every time you reveal through obedience what God has done in your life, it is as if shreds of flesh were being torn from your heart. This is quite true... When Jesus had his sweat of blood, his Divine Body was covered with countless wounds. That is why His Body was torn to shreds during the scourging. As for us, since we have reached an agreement, we shall continue this conversation.*

G.F. — Must I answer all your questions?

A.G. — *Yes, for this testimony goes in the sense of your offering to the Eternal Father when you told Him: Eternal Father, I offer you my life as a witness to the authenticity of the apparitions of the Blessed Virgin at Medjugorje.*

G.F. — I agree to answer your questions but I always have the impression that I am talking about another person.

A.G. — *Well, tell me, what were the first graces you received in your life?*

G.F. — At about the age of six I began to hear the voice of Jesus in my heart. I thought that this constant dialogue with Jesus was normal for all children...

A.G. — *You must have been happy to hear that voice!*

G.F. — Yes, but I have often wished not to hear that voice of Jesus anymore, for to remain faithful to Our Lord's requests is very demanding. Moreover, Satan would tell me that this was all fake (sheer invention)!

A.G. — *Did you speak of this to anyone?*

G.F. — No, because I was afraid of being ridiculed and my soul as a child was often in anguish. At that time, Satan used to tell me that I was damned... He would tell me: "You have made a bad confession... You have committed a sacrilege." I was torn and I often wept at the thought of having lost my Blessed Jesus and my friendship with the Virgin Mary. Nevertheless, I always took refuge in Her. It was only later that my soul as a child was enlightened.

A.G. — *For how long have you been hearing this voice of Jesus?*

G.F. — For 66 years.

A.G. — *You have, therefore, spoken much to Jesus!*

G.F. — Not only with Jesus, but also with the Father and the Holy Spirit and with the Most Blessed Virgin Mary as well.

A.G. — *You mean to say that you also hear the voice of the Eternal Father, the voice of the Holy Spirit... the voice of Mary.*

G.F. — Yes, that is so...

A.G. — *But how can you tell them apart?*

G.F. — The voice of the Divine Persons is sensed in the innermost depths of my heart, and also in my ear...

A.G. — *How do they address you?*

G.F. — They communicate with me in different words and expressions... The tone of the voice is also different.

A.G. — *How does the Eternal Father speak to you?*

G.F. — He speaks with more authority, but also with great love and great mercy. His voice is more solemn. I feel that a certain reverent but loving awe invades my heart, as the Father speaks to his child. As for Mary, He is the one who has authority over Her.

A.G. — *Can you speak in this sense about Jesus as well?*

G.F. — Jesus addresses me in a more personal language. He calls me: "My Beloved, My little Bride... My little host of love, My little victim of love." His language is one of gentleness and, if He chides me, he consoles me at the same time for the grief I feel.

A.G. — *And the Holy Spirit?*

G.F. — He especially helps me in the decisions I have to make. I feel deep within me that it is the Holy Spirit who directs my prayer. He helps me in everything, even in material tasks.

A.G. — *Do you understand very well that the persons of the Trinity are distinct?*

G.F. — Yes, I see it within me with a kind of evidence but I do not have the words to explain it. I also see that they make but one God.

A.G. — *You have told me that the Virgin Mary spoke to you. What role does She play in your life?*

G.F. — She is my Mother! I am Her daughter. She is part of my intimacy with God.

A.G. — *What does She talk about to you?*

G.F. — She speaks to me of the mercy of the Father towards me and towards mankind. She speaks to me of Her Son Jesus, of all He has suffered for me. She tells me to be very attentive to the graces of the Holy Spirit and to His inspirations. She is my confidante. She directs me to the Cross of Her Son as she shows me how to conform myself totally to the Will of the Father.

A.G. — *Does She do anything else for you?*

G.F. — Yes, Mary is the one who guides me in my spiritual life. She is the one who gives me formative training.

A.G. — *What do you mean by formative training?*

G.F. — She teaches me how to understand what God accomplishes in me. She teaches me humility; it is always with an infinite tact and a motherly gentleness that She admonishes me when I do not amend my failings.

A.G. — *Georgette, now I see how the three Divine Persons and the Virgin Mary have led you. Is there a priest who has guided you in your spiritual life?*

G.F. — I waited for almost twenty years before I found a priest, a spiritual director, who would find out about my life and have the grace to believe in it.

A.G. — *Who was this priest?*

G.F. — Father Joseph Gamache, S.J., was my spiritual director for twenty (20) years. He passed away at the age of eighty-four (84).

A.G. — *And after his death?*

G.F. — Father Paul Mayer, S.J., was my second spiritual director. He is now eighty-four (84) years old. He directed me for 17 years. He was the one who asked me to pray so that the Eternal Father would clearly show me the one who should be my new spiritual director. He asked me to make a three-day retreat for that purpose...

A.G. — *When did you find out?*

G.F. — I did not want to choose one according to my personal inclinations. I prayed very much and on December 8, 1983, on the feast of the Immaculate Conception, during the celebration of the Holy Mass, I clearly heard the Virgin Mary indicating the very specific choice of the Eternal Father. *"Father Armand will be your spiritual director and Father Guy Girard will be your spiritual counsellor and will be responsible for your spiritual notes."*

A.G. — *Very well, Georgette, but do you believe that other people can hear this inner voice?*

G.F. — Yes, I am convinced of that. I am not a person specially set aside. We must be attentive to the inspirations of grace which we receive in prayer, and in silence be constantly asking the Blessed Virgin to lead us to the Father with Jesus.

We must not seek the marvellous. It is in the simplicity of the heart, the soul and the spirit that God manifests himself. We must humbly ask the Virgin Mary to teach us how to love and serve the Father. The soul which asks with Faith and sincerity is always answered. Never does the Father reject a prayer! He chooses his hour! We must be ready to wait...

Spiritual Ascent

A.G. — *Obviously, prayer is the road we must travel to reach intimacy with the divine. Georgette, you have journeyed through this spiritual ascent which has not yet come to an end. I would like to ask you a few questions. When you were young, how did you pray?*

G.F. — One of the first incidents which challenged me was the following one. When I injured myself at the age of four, my grandmother asked me to unite my suffering to that of Jesus. She would say: "Look at Jesus. He has not only one finger which is hurting but his whole hand." I would kiss the crucifix and say to my grandmother: "This hurts just the same!" Meanwhile, I always grew up with this inner voice speaking to me. It was something absolutely normal for me. I did not attach any importance to it. I liked to go and pray in solitude and quiet. It was then that the dialogue with Jesus was more intimate.

A.G. — *How much time did you devote to prayer?*

G.F. — Prayer was my refuge in joy as in grief. I would ask the Eternal Father to protect me. I would devote as much time as possible to it. When I was about 15, I would make at least one holy hour each day.

A.G. — *Don't you believe that the length of time you devoted to prayer was exaggerated?*

G.F. — No, I don't think so. To give one out of 24 hours is not exaggerated. God takes care of us 24 hours a day.

A.G. — *Were there other means that helped you in your spiritual journey?*

G.F. — Yes, I had consecrated myself to Mary in the Congregation of the Children of Mary.

A.G. — *Something else, possibly?*

G.F. — Yes, at 17, I offered myself as a victim to the Merciful Love for the salvation of the world. This was a group called: "The Association of Victim Souls" for which Father Charette, a Dominican, was responsible.

A.G. — *Did you make any vows?*

G.F. — Yes, I made the three vows (poverty, chastity, obedience) in the presence of my spiritual director, Father Gamache, S.J.

A.G. — *Did you then make any other vows?*

G.F. — Yes, my director asked me if I was willing to make the vow of immolation and offer myself as a sacrifice of Love to the Eternal Father for consecrated souls. This I did with joy. Later Jesus spoke to me of a spiritual betrothal.

A.G. — *Did you know what this meant?*

G.F. — I understood it from what Jesus was telling me. But I always knew myself to be unworthy. It seemed to me that this was only for consecrated men and women.

A.G. — *When did Jesus ask you to become His Betrothed?*

G.F. — On February 22, 1953. *I want you as my betrothed,* he said to me. *And you will wear the ring that your spiritual director will bless. This ring will always protect you. It will help you to fulfill your role as the betrothed of Christ and to be faithful to it. You, you are nothing. As for Me, I am everything.*

A.G. — *Was this commitment demanding for you?*

G.F. — Yes, a greater demand for prayer in order to respond to what God expects of me. But, I had moments of rebellion when

I removed my ring and threw it away for I did not want to have anything to do with Jesus's demands anymore.

A.G. — *What was Jesus's reaction?*

G.F. — Jesus was hurt by this vile gesture of revolt. His heart was wounded because of all that He had done for me. He would tell me: *"With what love I leaned over you when you were wounded by sin!"* Jesus then leaned over me with much more love and care.

A.G. — *How did you live after that period of revolt?*

G.F. — It was a period of aridity, struggles, attacks from Satan who wanted to destroy me. "You have no reason to keep on living", Satan would tell me. I felt no more attraction for prayer. Even the sacraments had become a burden for me. My spiritual director wearied me. It seemed to me that he had become an obstacle to my spiritual life.

A.G. — *And then?*

G.F. — Then, my spiritual director compelled me to write all that I was experiencing in order to check more closely my spiritual life and all that my hidden intimacy contained. This was painful to me for I felt I was betraying a secret which I had shared with Jesus and Mary ever since my childhood. These were difficult moments. This hidden intimacy was known to no one then. I experienced a feeling of betrayal. I felt guilty even when I spoke of this to my spiritual director. But one day, the Lord told me: *"Tell him everything, he represents Me."*

I did not believe that suffering united to that of Jesus had the dimension of redemption and purification. I perceived suffering as a punishment.

A.G. — *How did you perceive God?*

G.F. — I felt He was remote. I did not want to see a crucifix anymore. His wounds turned me away from Him. In the state of soul I was in, I did not believe anymore that this was purification. I did not believe what Father Gamache, my spiritual director, told me anymore. One day, this priest said: "Your soul cost the

Blood of Christ and it is costing me much as well.'' It was only later that I understood what that priest had done in prayer, self-denial, fasting to help me and to liberate my soul. He was the one who made me respond to what God was expecting of me.

A.G. — *After this spiritual journey, what did God ask you to do?*

G.F. — He asked me to sever myself from my family, my surroundings, my friends and He led me to renounce my will. This was the most important: to sever myself from myself.

A.G. — *What does all this self-denial represent for you?*

G.F. — It makes me realize that without God I can do nothing. It makes me understand his infinite Mercy, for I can see Him, His arms stretched out towards us to receive us whatever be the state of our souls. I see Him blind to our sins, our failings, His Heart full of love always ready to accept us. All He asks of a soul is good will, sincerity, trust in His Infinite Mercy for each one of us. What is most important is conformity to the Will of the Father in all things and in all places, as Jesus and Mary achieved it!

A.G. — *How do you understand the vow as priest and victim which you made some time ago?*

G.F. — This vow is the culminating point of all my life. I recall that since the age of four, I have always felt suffering in my body. From this day onward, Jesus is inviting me to identify myself with Him as priest and victim in the perfect and full development of royal priesthood. Jesus made me grasp the fact that Holy Mass is not primarily a meal, but that it is the ultimate sacrifice of Jesus dying on the cross for the salvation of the world. At the moment of the consecration, I unite myself to the sacrificial Lamb. The Eucharist is the source of my strength.

A.G. — *And so life goes on?*

G.F. — You know that. You are in a good position to know this.

A.G. — *Very well, Georgette, thank you!*

The Wounds of Jesus

A.G. — *You know, Georgette, I have the impression that each one of my questions is a wound in your heart. But, tell me, nevertheless, something about the wounds of Jesus hidden in your body. Since when do you have them?*

G.F. — In 1950, Jesus made me understand that I had His Most Holy Wounds.

A.G. — *Do you have the wounds of Jesus's hands and feet?*

G.F. — Yes, I have them. The Father gave them to me as a pure gift and I feel very unworthy of having them.

A.G. — *Precisely, where is the pain of the hands of Jesus located?*

G.F. — The nails to support the body of Jesus on the cross were driven through the wrists. This is where the pains are the most acute and the most intense.

A.G. — *And the feet?*

G.F. — No, it is a little different for the feet. When I am lying down, I always have my feet one on top of the other.

A.G. — *Where are the wounds in the feet?*

G.F. — They are on the side, the left foot supports the right foot. When the Lord asks for much suffering, He is the One who places my feet.

A.G. — *And the crown of thorns?*

G.F. — I received it on April 25, 1953. Jesus told me on that day: *Today I am setting my crown of thorns on your head.*

A.G. — *Did you have difficulty in accepting it?*

G.F. — No, I am not worthy of it, but I accepted that the Will of God be done.

A.G. — *Is it always more or less painful?*

G.F. — It is much more painful on Fridays for two reasons: because it is the day of the Lord's death, and the other reason depends on what Jesus demands.

A.G. — *Did the medical doctors try to find where the pains come from?*

G.F. — Yes, but the doctors found nothing! When the Lord chooses a victim soul for himself, neither the doctors nor science can find the source and the intensity of the pains to nurse them. Jesus told me: *It is only after your death that doctors will be able to know the pains that you have borne.*

A.G. — *What about the wound of the pierced heart of Jesus?*

G.F. — The wound of the Heart of Jesus is a persistent pain which never stops, but the wound on the shoulder is the most painful.

A.G. — *People never speak of that wound on the shoulder.*

G.F. — I know but, precisely, this sixth wound that Jesus had, is very painful. Jesus is the one who showed me that the wound of the shoulder was the most painful of all during the carrying of the cross. It was after considerable research that my spiritual director, Father Joseph Gamache, S.J., discovered that the existence of the sixth wound located on the shoulder had been revealed to Saint Bernard. *While carrying the cross I had a wound three fingers deep and three bones were laid bare on my shoulder.*

A.G. — *Did you ask on which shoulder was this wound?*

G.F. — Yes, I asked Jesus and he told me: *I was carrying the cross on my left shoulder (on the side of the heart) in order to keep my right hand free to bless my people a last time.*

A.G. — *Would you add anything else to these answers?*

G.F. — Yes, I would say that the interior sufferings of Jesus were greater than his physical sufferings. *My soul is sad unto death,* He sighed. He was experiencing the agony of the soul, the heart and the spirit. The heart of Jesus was wounded by the ingratitude of men. Jesus died of having loved too much! His

73

Heart was opened by love even before the soldier pierced it to check if He was dead. This was but a symbolic gesture.

A.G. — *Thank you, Georgette, for these findings.*

The Alliance

A.G. — *Georgette, you have already spoken to me about a mark made by God on your body. Could you tell me something more about this manifestation of God towards you?*

G.F. — I have already told you that it is not easy for me to answer your questions but I promised that I would do so. Yes, on February 2, 1982, on the feast of the Purification, the Lord asked me to offer more suffering for the Holy Father, for the consecrated souls, and to accept to bear the sins of mankind.

A.G. — *What happened then?*

G.F. — I agreed to everything, but I had only the usual suffering. I found myself and always find myself unworthy of bearing the sins of mankind when I am a sinner myself.

A.G. — *And then?*

G.F. — On Good Friday 1982, I had much more suffering. It was in these great pains that God was manifesting himself. Through his grace, I understood the importance of what God had demanded of me on February 2, 1982.

A.G. — *Then?*

G.F. — On July 1, 1982, on the feast of the Precious Blood, God manifested himself for the third time by renewing his request.

A.G. — *How? By words or by signs?*

G.F. — God was manifesting his request by a sharp pain on the right side and by leaving a mark in my flesh in the shape of the number two. As I looked, I saw a red spot in the shape of a two in which blood was circulating normally.

A.G. — *Did you speak of this manifestation of God to your spiritual director?*

G.F. — Yes, I confided to him what was happening to me.

A.G. — *And your director?*

G.F. — Then my director asked me if I knew the meaning of what was happening to me. As I was saying no for the second time, Jesus intervened: *You will answer your director: Now we are two in one same flesh.*

A.G. — *Did you say that to your director?*

G.F. — Yes, I had to say it.

A.G. — *And he?*

G.F. — Then my director replied: "If that is so, you have not come to the end of your suffering!" And he added: "Thank the Lord, you have received a great favor."

A.G. — *After that, was there greater suffering?*

G.F. — Yes, greater suffering was felt on the right side, but only when there was a very specific reason.

A.G. — *Did your director demand a proof of this manifestation?*

G.F. — Yes, he asked me to have it checked by a physician and to have a photo taken of it.

A.G. — *Did the doctor do the checking as had been requested?*

G.F. — Yes, the doctor checked it. He had to kneel to see it better. Jesus was making me know that the doctor had to kneel to see the sign of God inlaid in my flesh. Fearing that this was my imagination at work, I did not dare ask him to kneel down. Then I asked Jesus to inspire him to kneel down. At the moment I was asking him, he knelt and saw the shape of the two perfectly.

A.G. — *What was his reaction?*

G.F. — He was amazed when he examined it with a magnifying glass while telling me: "As a doctor, I have never seen a sign like this. It is unbelievable; this sign looks like a luminous neon where we can see the blood circulating, blood that is perfectly synchronized with the beating of the heart, and yet it is not linked with any adjacent organ. I see it very well even if the number is very small."

A.G. — *Was a photo taken as requested by your spiritual director?*

G.F. — Yes, photos were taken, but without any results. When I spoke to my director, he said: "I am asking you to try one last time. If the photo is not a success, this is an indication that God does not wish this sign impressed in your flesh to be seen. This is, therefore, the last authorization I am giving you."

A.G. — *Did the last photo give any results?*

G.F. — Yes, the photo was taken by another doctor who used the hospital camera. This camera was equipped with a magnifying lens. This photo was a perfect success, but this doctor also had to take it while kneeling.

A.G. — *Why must they kneel to take this photo?*

G.F. — Out of respect for the meaning of this sign: TWO IN ONE SAME FLESH.

A.G. — *What did the photo reveal?*

G.F. — It clearly revealed the presence of blood in the number two. This number is made up of seven red dots.

A.G. — *What is the meaning of the seven red dots?*

G.F. — They mean the seven gifts of the Holy Spirit. Now that several months have gone by, Jesus told me: *Henceforth, the number two must be called the ALLIANCE.*

A.G. — *Why did Jesus want it so?*

G.F. — Because the ALLIANCE shows the intimacy of God

with the soul and it also means a greater identification with the suffering of the crucified Christ. We will never be able to imagine the extent to which God loves us.

A.G. — *For how long have you had this ALLIANCE?*

G.F. — It was five years on July 1, 1987 since the AL-LIANCE, however fragile, has remained inlaid in my flesh.

A.G. — *The 1st of July is the Feast of the Precious Blood!*

G.F. — Yes, and Jesus shows me that the suffering I bear must identify me with Christ, priest and victim, to help the Holy Father, the consecrated souls, the Church and all of mankind.

A.G. — *Did you ask Jesus any other questions about the ALLIANCE?*

G.F. — Jesus made me understand not to ask any questions out of sheer curiosity. But he told me that this grace of the ALLIANCE is unique in the world.

A.G. — *Thank you, Georgette, for having revealed this to me.*

The Transfixion

A.G. — *Georgette, one day, during the celebration of the Eucharist, at the moment you received the Precious Blood of Christ, I saw your face full of suffering and your hands were clasped over your heart. What was going on?*

G.F. — I had a sharp pain in my heart.

A.G. — *Does this happen often?*

G.F. — Yes, it often happens during the day, sometimes during the night and also while I am working.

A.G. — *What is this pain like?*

G.F. — It is like a deep wound.

A.G. — *Can you describe this wound to me?*

G.F. — It is like a burning arrow of fire piercing my heart. The pain is extremely intense and increases when this arrow or dart is drawn out.

A.G. — *What happens then?*

G.F. — I feel my soul must never cease giving thanks while Jesus is wounding my heart. I thank Him for this suffering and I offer it to Him. At that moment, there is a very great interior joy in my soul. The greatest joys of the world cannot compare with what I feel within myself.

A.G. — *For whom do you offer this suffering?*

G.F. — I constantly offer this indescribable suffering to the Father in union with Jesus and Mary for the Holy Father, for the consecrated souls and for the whole Church.

A.G. — *Do you wish to have that wound?*

G.F. — Yes, I want it but I do not ask for it. I want to protect myself from all self-seeking. Jesus knows that in the innermost depths of myself, I want it. This wound makes me more like Jesus crucified.

A.G. — *How is that? Why does it make you more like Jesus crucified?*

G.F. — Because I unite my will to that of the Father as Jesus did all his life, but especially on the cross.

A.G. — *Are there any moments when these wounds are more painful and cause greater suffering?*

G.F. — On Fridays, and when God the Father asks for more suffering for the needs of the Church.

A.G. — *Does the Father ask you to offer these wounds for specific persons?*

G.F. — Yes, for the Holy Father, for the consecrated souls, for the priests of Medjugorje, for the boys and girls who see the Blessed Virgin, so that they will be protected from their enemies, visible and invisible, for the bishops of Yugoslavia, as well as for all those who recommend themselves to our prayers.

A.G. — *Does the Eternal Father ask for prayers for the apparitions of Medjugorje every day?*

G.F. — Yes, and I assume it upon myself as a duty. Since I heard of Medjugorje, I pray and offer my suffering so that the authenticity of the apparitions may be recognized as quickly as possible.

A.G. — *Do you offer these wounds of the heart for any other intentions?*

G.F. — Yes, I offer them so that the message of Mary, Queen of Peace, may be spread in all its authenticity throughout the whole world. Mary's message brings peace to souls and does not trouble them. The Most Blessed Virgin Mary never troubles souls. She always wants to lead them to the Heart of Jesus and to the Heart of the Father.

A.G. — *Are these wounds primarily a grace for yourself?*

G.F. — Yes, a very great grace! But we must not forget that Jesus has given his most holy wounds to the world, and that it is by these wounds that we are healed.

As for myself, I share these wounds of the heart with the souls God entrusts to me especially those of the priests and the consecrated.

A.G. — *Do you know the prayer of Saint John of the Cross concerning these wounds of the heart?*

G.F. — No, but I would like to know it to recite it.

A.G. — *It is most beautiful! Here it is:*

> *"Lord, wound me with a wound of love which may be healed only by being wounded again."*

G.F. — Thank you. Saint John of the Cross expressed this very well. From now on, I will be able to recite it.

Visions

A.G. — *I know that you do not like to speak about certain favors you have received, but I have a moral obligation in writing this testimony and I must ask you other questions. Georgette, have you ever been favored with VISIONS?*

G.F. — I have occasionally had inner visions but these moments of my life have always brought me very great suffering.

A.G. — *Why do these inner visions cause suffering for you?*

G.F. — When I saw Jesus crucified, wearing his crown of thorns, I wept over my numerous sins, over the sins of the whole world.

A.G. — *Would you like to tell me more about this vision?*

G.F. — This inner vision is to ask me to unite myself more to Jesus on the Cross and to share His suffering and the sorrows of Mary.

A.G. — *Did you see the Virgin Mary in a vision?*

G.F. — Yes. I saw Her in an inner vision. I saw her weeping because of her priests, her favorite sons. That is beyond description. It is like an image which impints itself in my soul. It can never be forgotten.

A.G. — *Since you have heard about Medjugorje, have you had inner visions of the Virgin Mary concerning these apparitions?*

G.F. — Yes, one day after I had prayed that these apparitions might be recognized and that the obstacles might disappear, I saw the Virgin Mary weeping.

A.G. — *What did you feel?*

G.F. — I felt grief. I was convinced that She was weeping because of the situation at Medjugorje.

A.G. — *Can one imagine hearing her weep?*

G.F. — It is not imagination. When I hear Her weeping because of her consecrated souls, *her tears are sobs, they are like a physical pain.*

A.G. — *Is it the same in the case of Medjugorje?*

G.F. — No, in the case of Medjugorje, I did not hear *sobs as it were.* She was weeping profusely, but in the silence and the dignity of a mother and of a Queen.

A.G. — *Can you explain to me the content of the visions which are linked with Medjugorje?*

G.F. — In these visions, I see the Virgin Mary. She is earnestly asking for prayers for the priests of Medjugorje, but also for the priests who visit this holy place, for the pilgrims and the visionaries, so that they may remain faithful to what the Virgin Mary asks of them.

A.G. — *Are there other requests?*

G.F. — Yes, at the time of these visions, one request of the Virgin Mary is very explicit and is made with much insistence. She asks to pray so that the Church may recognize, through the power of the Holy Spirit, the authenticity of the apparitions for the glory of the Father and that of Jesus.

A.G. — *Have you anything else to add to what you have just told me?*

G.F. — Yes. Mary's requests involve the FIDELITY of the villagers to PRAYER, to the EUCHARIST, to FASTING, to the ROSARY, and to the SACRAMENT OF RECONCILIATION. This fidelity can only promote a greater fidelity to Mary's requests among the pilgrims.

A.G. — *Did you have other visions?*

G.F. — I saw the Holy Father John Paul II experience a very great loneliness. I remember the day of his election when He was telling the world: "Do not be afraid", a woman I was with said: "This Polish Pope, young and exceptionally healthy, will live a long time." But I distinctly heard in my heart and in my ear:

81

"He is young, but men will make a prematurely aged man of him."

A.G. — *What is the content of the other visions?*

G.F. — I have already answered that! It is about the Holy Father John Paul II. The Virgin Mary wants to make me understand to pray more for him because of the great responsibility he bears: that of leading the people of God to the Father.

A.G. — *Do the inner visions have other purposes?*

G.F. — Yes, through these visions, the Virgin Mary is asking me to pray for certain events which are happening in the world. She is also asking me to pray for people who are victims of natural disasters, or the wickedness of men, injustice, or violence. All these evils are rooted in pride.

We must humbly ask the Eternal Father to change our hearts by a greater love for God and for our neighbor. This intercession must always be made in the faith and trust that our prayer can be answered.

A.G. — *Georgette, these confidences you are sharing with us invite us to perseverance in prayer. Mankind needs this air to revitalize it. Thank you for this!*

The Gift of Tongues

G.G. — *Georgette, I know that my brother Armand has "tortured" you enough with his questions. In spite of that, I would also like to ask a few. I notice that people are very eager to see you. Why?*

G.F. — They come for advice or for help.

G.G. — *Do you welcome them willingly?*

G.F. — Yes. Jesus told me: *"Welcome all the people whom I will send to you. Greet them as if they were Myself.*

G.G. — *You tell me you help them. In what way?*

G.F. — The Holy Spirit inspires me only when I am in the presence of the person; I begin to relate a fact in which the person concerned recognizes himself. What God wants me to describe is often a situation identical to the problem presented.

G.G. — *Can we say that you have the power of reading in souls?*

G.F. — No. The Holy Spirit does not reveal the state of souls to me. However, He can give me a feeling of the state of a soul, that is, of grief, anxiety, fear, worry. All that stems from the lack of faith, of surrender to the Father's Will. God can also allow these states to be a purification for the soul. Then the Holy Spirit indicates that to me. He tells me so. Satan can suggest, but he cannot inspire. Hence, the necessity to discern. This discernment, which is a sheer gift of God, is given to me to see through the situation clearly.

G.G. — *Do you pray during these encounters with people?*

G.F. — Yes. While I am speaking to these people, my heart remains in a state of prayer; my soul can rise toward God while I remain attentive to the problem they are talking about.

G.G. — *Can you say that you live two kinds of presence?*

G.F. — Yes, an invisible one, that is, the presence to the Holy Spirit. The other, visible, is the presence to the person. It is like the real Presence. I look at the host which is a visible presence at the human level and a real presence at the supernatural level. That can be explained only through faith.

G.G. — *Who are the people who come to see you most frequently?*

G.F. — All kinds of people. There are poor, wealthy, well educated, illiterate people. But often they are abandoned people who are feeling their own way and seeking God without being aware of it. There are also consecrated souls. But I especially like children. I feel at ease when talking to them about Jesus and Mary.

G.G. — *Why do you like children better?*

G.F. — Because they are simple. They like to hear people talking about God. They always seek to know more. So when we speak of Jesus, of Mary, of the Trinity, they accept them without any discussion for they have no pride. God cannot refuse to answer their prayers. The Holy Spirit works in their hearts and makes them want to know more about Jesus and Mary. When you explain the love of God, the love of Jesus for them, they grasp this very well. They really feel they are loved and they are happy. We see there the importance of the religious education that the parents must pass on to their children at a very early age.

G.G. — *Do you often receive priests?*

G.F. — Yes. Jesus told me to receive them with an open heart and a great deal of charity. *Receive them through the love I put in you.*

G.G. — *Whom do you see in the priests who come to you?*

G.F. — I see the representatives of God. But often I see them as wounded souls who need help, especially prayers. Every day I place them in the arms of Mary, Queen of Peace, so that they may find peace of soul, heart and mind, and thus discover the FAITH they must have in their PRIESTHOOD.

G.G. — *When your visitors do not speak French, can you receive them?*

G.F. — Yes, for Jesus helps me. There are interpreters sometimes but if they have not rendered or translated their questions well, Jesus tells me exactly what I must understand.

G.G. — *Give me an example of that.*

G.F. — One day, I received a Spanish-speaking lady and the interpreter had not yet arrived. When she spoke to me in Spanish, Jesus made me understand her in French. When I spoke to her in French, she understood me in Spanish. When the interpreter arrived, the meeting was over and he was wondering to himself: "Why did you ask me to come?"

G.G. — *Does this happen in other languages?*

G.F. — Yes, as this happened in Spanish. Jesus would help me in other languages.

G.G. — *For you, Georgette, this is a particular gift!*

G.F. — I am always grateful to God for the gifts I receive in sheer gratuity. Encounters of this type, which He allows me to have, always bring good results because He is there to help us.

G.G. — *Thanks be to God.*

The Croatian Language and the Hymn "Mirtha o Mirtha"

G.G. — *We know, Georgette, that you do not speak any other language but French. But do you sometimes recite prayers in languages other than French?*

G.F. — Yes, I recite prayers in Latin like the "Pater", the "Ave Maria", the "Gloria Patri".

G.G. — *Do you sing in Latin?*

G.F. — Yes. Often during thanksgiving, after the Holy Eucharist, I sing the "Magnificat", the "Salve Regina", the "Ave Maria".

G.G. — *Does it not sometimes happen to you that you answer prayers or that you sing in a language unknown to you?*

G.F. — Yes, this has often happened for the last three years. You are with me and sometimes with your brother Father Armand. You have told me that I answer the "Hail Mary" and other prayers in another language.

G.G. — *That is true. I am a witness of that and Father Armand as well. But can you tell me in what language you recite or sing these prayers?*

G.F. — No. All I can say is that this is beyond my control. The Lord leads me to answer or to sing in another language. It is like a voice unknown to me. I hear the words within myself and in my ear. I say them or I sing them as I hear them.

G.G. — *Have you ever asked the Eternal Father in what language you are praying or singing when that manifests itself?*

G.F. — Yes. Your brother Father Armand asked me to question the Eternal Father on that when he was preparing to celebrate the Holy Eucharist.

G.G. — *Can you say when and how the question was asked?*

G.F. — It was on January 24, 1986. At each celebration of the Eucharist we pray that the apparitions of the Virgin Mary at Medjugorje be recognized. So we thought it was Croatian. The question was formulated in this manner: "Most Holy Father, why do you allow your servant to pray in Croatian?"

G.G. — *Did the Eternal Father give an answer?*

G.F. — Yes, the answer of the Eternal Father was very clear in my heart and in my ear. He answered me: *Offer in sacrifice the fact of not having an answer immediately. Offer that sacrifice to help Vicka go through the trial which is demanded of her. Offer it as well to help the other visionaries in their journey of faith.*

G.G. — *How did you understand this answer?*

G.F. — I understood that the Eternal Father would give us an answer at the time He Himself would choose.

G.G. — *Did you receive this answer?*

G.F. — Yes, we received it on February 26, 1986.

G.G. — *What is the answer of the Eternal Father?*

G.F. — The Eternal Father gave me an answer which deals first with a hymn. Often this hymn rises in my heart during the act of thanksgiving. The first words are MIRTHA O MIRTHA.

G.G. — *What did He say concerning this hymn?*

G.F. — He said: *The hymn MIRTHA O MIRTHA, which can also be a RECITED PRAYER*[1], is in Croatian.

G.G. — *I would like to question you more on this hymn "MIRTHA O MIRTHA", but let us go back to recited prayers. Did you ask the Eternal Father what language was used in recited prayers and in spontaneous prayers?*

G.F. — Yes, it was on Friday, the 28th of February 1986 during the Eucharist that the Eternal Father gave me the answer.

G.G. — *What is that answer?*

G.F. — The Eternal Father told me: *The prayers you are reciting are in Aramaean.* And I replied to Him: "Even the 'Hail Mary'? And the Eternal Father answered: *Especially the 'Hail Mary'."*

G.G. — *For what reason?*

G.F. — To render homage to the Queen of Peace, our Mother, Mother of the Church.

G.G. — *What are the prayers most frequently recited in Aramaean?*

G.F. — They are the "Our Father", the "Hail Mary", the "Glory be to the Father", the "I believe in God".

G.G. — *When you are by yourself, do you pray also in Aramaean?*

G.F. — I do not know, but I sometimes pray in a strange language unknown to me.

G.G. — *I would like you to recall for me what happened concerning the prayers.*

G.F. — Yes, you remember one day you had brought a brochure in which there were prayers in Croatian. You wanted to check without my being aware of it if I was praying in Croatian. We began to pray. As soon as we began, the Lord warned me

---

1. See Appendix 1, page 91.

of your intentions and asked me to reprimand you. I did so and you asked the Eternal Father to forgive you.

G.G. — *Thank you for this very meaningful reminder! Now, let us come back to the prayers. We know why the Eternal Father makes you recite the "Hail Mary" in Aramaean. You have answered that question. But, is the reason the same for the other prayers?*

G.F. — No, the Eternal Father told me: *They are said in reparation for the prayers which are distorted in the Church. This is the reason why I ask you to recite these prayers in reparation for the wound made to the heart of Jesus and Mary.*

G.G. — *Did the Eternal Father give the reason for the hymn MIRTHA O MIRTHA in Croatian and the prayers in Aramaean?*

G.F. — Yes, and the answer is most beautiful. The hymn in CROATIAN renders homage to the Eternal Father through Mary. The prayers in ARAMAEAN render homage to JESUS and to MARY.

G.G. — *Let us go back to the hymn MIRTHA O MIRTHA. On February 26, 1986, the Eternal Father said that this hymn is in Croatian. Do you sing it when you are alone by yourself?*

G.F. — Yes, I sometimes sing it when I am alone, but especially when you are here for the Mass and for thanksgiving, or with Father Armand. This happens more when you are both here for the celebration of the Holy Eucharist and thanksgiving.

G.G. — *How was this hymn given?*

G.F. — I hear it in my heart and in my ear. I have the words and I sing them as I hear them. But it is evident that without the help of the Virgin Mary, I would not be able to sing anything. I am but a very poor instrument which She is willing to use.

G.G. — *How do you explain the help of the Virgin Mary? How do you perceive it?*

G.F. — When I think of my illness (oppression, angina, pulmonary infection, dizziness, etc...), my condition of extreme weakness, it is physically impossible for me to sing. So when I do so, it is the Virgin Mary who is helping me. I have no merit whatsoever for I clearly perceive that this voice which sings is totally strange to me. I perceive this voice, very soft, very young. I really am aware that Mary uses me, the poor servant that I am, to praise the Eternal Father.

G.G. — *Why did the Eternal Father give you this hymn?*

G.F. — He gave me this hymn because it is the hymn that the Virgin Mary sings

> — to magnify the Eternal Father
> — and to give peace to the world.

G.G. — *Has the Eternal Father said anything else about this hymn?*

G.F. — Yes. He said: *I offer this hymn or this prayer as a GIFT TO THE PARISH OF MEDJUGORJE.* He asked that the translation be made in Croatian by the author of the book "Je vois la Vierge". And He clearly gave the name of this priest.[2]

G.G. — *What else is there about this hymn?*

G.F. — The Eternal Father also said that this hymn was given out of GRATITUDE for all the LOVE, the RESPECT and the FIDELITY of Medjugorje to and for the Queen of Peace.

G.G. — *Can you sum up what happened after we received the translation of this hymn?*

G.F. — Yes, on February 24, 1986, we had the complete translation of the hymn MIRTHA O MIRTHA.[3]
On February 25, 1986, the Eternal Father said that the prayers are in the language of the early Church.

G.G. — *How is the hymn MIRTHA O MIRTHA from the musical point of view?*

---

2. Father Janko Bubalo.
3. See Appendices 1 and 2, p. 91 and pp. 92-93.

G.F. — On March 1, 1986, the Holy Spirit inspired the musical notation of the hymn to me.

G.G. — *How was that done?*

G.F. — I could hear the melody, so I wrote it according to the wish of the Eternal Father. For thirty-three years I had given up music. But it was easy for me to write this because the Holy Spirit showed me the notation. Father Armand was present.

G.G. — *This melody is marvelous and we must thank God for such a gift. The Eternal Father in his infinite kindness has created an alliance between Medjugorje and Montreal for the joy of Mary.*

Appendix 1

MIRTHA O MIRTHA

Peace, o gentle Peace,
be our constant hope.
Queen of the Peace,
accept our praise.
From all dangers, protect us all!
In our combats, remain with us!
To magnify the Eternal Father,
give all of us your love.
O Blessed Trinity, with our Mother,
let us proclaim your Mercy,
the power of Your Eternal Love.
Queen of the Peace, hear the prayer
of your children of the earth
beseeching you to give them Peace.

Appendix 2

It appears necessary to me to add a long commentary in order to make experiences, past and present, very clear to the reader.

Firstly

When we speak of the hymn in Croatian heard here in Canada, more precisely in Montreal, we are speaking of the melody and the words. This hymn which the "Virgin Mary" sings

— to magnify the Eternal Father
— and to give peace to the world,

is sung by Georgette. It is in Croatian as has been mentioned. However, this Croatian is not comprehensible. We had two Croatian-speaking Yugoslavians listen to a recording of it. They can hear the words, but they do not understand what they mean. When we were in Medjugorje in October 1986, Father JANKO BUBALO asked for other explanations about the Croatian language of that hymn. Father Armand Girard phoned from CITLUCK (Yugoslavia) on October 15, 1986 to Georgette Faniel (Montreal, Canada).

The servant of the Eternal Father answered: "The Eternal Father has already given us an answer to that." Nevertheless, she prayed and the Eternal Father told her: *This is an ancient Croatian language which they would not be able to understand.*

It is a miracle of LOVE which no one will be able to understand. It is a hymn from heaven.[1]

Secondly

We know that this hymn is a gift from the Eternal Father to the parish of Medjugorje in two ways.

The *first way* is by the TRANSLATION of it. The Eternal Father gave the translation of this hymn MIRTHA Ô MIRTHA which may be used as a recited prayer. It is the beautiful prayer: "Peace, ô gentle Peace".[2] Father JANKO BUBALO is to translate this prayer into Croatian and this is the prayer for peace they will recite at Medjugorje.

The *second way* is by the MELODY. Father JANKO BUBALO writes what follows: "While listening to the melody of this hymn, I noticed something EXTRAORDINARY, that is, that the TUNE of this hymn is IDENTICAL with that of my hymn 'Before Our Lady' composed by a Franciscan from BOSNIA, Father SLAVKO TOPIĆ. The difference lies only in the BEAT and the KEYS. As was suggested by the Fathers Girard, the melody is reproduced at the end of the book with the words from Father JANKO BUBALO and the *music* from Georgette Faniel".[3]

Not only do the words of Father JANKO BUBALO totally agree with the inspired melody, but this melody adds considerable merit to the words of Father Bubalo.

That a melody written by two different persons be identical when they do not know each other, do not speak the same language, and are thousands of miles distant from each other is a sign of the Love of the Eternal Father. The intervention of God is manifest.

Father Guy Girard, S.SS.A.

---

1. VICKA, speaking of the HEAVEN that the Virgin Mary made her see with JAKOV, says: "The elect were happy, joyful. They were singing and speaking among themselves in a language which we did not understand" (René Laurentin, *Medjugorje, récit et message des apparitions,* O.E.I.L., 1986, p. 91).

2. See Appendix 1, p. 91.

3. See p. 227.

The Eternal Father

G.G. — *Georgette, we know from the Gospel that Jesus spent long hours in prayer in the intimacy of the Eternal Father. In my conversations with you, I became aware that there was a very strong emphasis placed on the Eternal Father in your spiritual life. Could you speak more to us about this hidden treasure? But, first, since when do you have this devotion?*

G.F. — This devotion to the Eternal Father is central to my life. But it was not so in my childhood. This devotion came later.

G.G. — *Can you explain how this devotion developed?*

G.F. — When I was preparing to make my first communion, I began to hear the voice of Jesus. I thought it was like this for all children.

G.G. — *And the voice of the Father, you could hear it?*

G.F. — No, this came much later.

G.G. — *Did you hear the voice of the Most Blessed Virgin Mary?*

G.F. — Yes, when I was about 12, I could hear the voice of Mary. If She made any demands from me, they were for specific intentions. She would speak to me of Jesus, his love for me and for each human being. She would speak to me of the Father and his infinite mercy. She would give me advice.

G.G. — *What advice did She give you?*

G.F. — She would ask me to be attentive to the Holy Spirit, to pray to Her in difficult moments. She would ask me to amend my shortcomings.

G.G. — *What did She tell you to make you more attentive to the Holy Spirit?*

G.F. — She would tell me to read over often all the gifts received in Confirmation. I would reread in the catechism the parts concerning the gifts of the Holy Spirit. I tried to put them into practice. For example, during tests in school, etc...

G.G. — *How did you pray Her in difficult moments?*

G.F. — Inwardly, I would draw nearer to Her. I would take a small statue of the Blessed Virgin. I would kiss it in tears because I feared I had hurt Her or Jesus.

G.G. — *Why did you cry?*

G.F. — I was becoming more aware that my failings caused them grief. For example, if I quarrelled with my brothers and sisters, I would ask Jesus and Mary to forgive me. Mary would ask me to apologize to them. She would show me very clearly how to amend my ways. When I would fall again because of my shortcomings, the Virgin Mary would suggest that I make sacrifices: go without desserts, sweets, etc... She would often urge me to be patient.

G.G. — *You were telling me, a few moments ago, that your devotion to the Eternal Father developed much later. Can you tell me what was Mary's role in this devotion?*

G.F. — The Virgin Mary was leading me to the Eternal Father.

G.G. — *In what way?*

G.F. — She made me accept the Father's Will on many occasions, among others, accept my illness, give up music lessons because of my ill health, and also trips with my parents for the same reason. She was preparing my soul for total detachment and liberating it for prayer and quiet recollection.

G.G. — *What else?*

G.F. — She made me understand the Father's love and mercy, for I did not know Him well. It is thanks to Mary that I understood his boundless tenderness and his infinite patience. I have always asked the Blessed Virgin to lead me to the Father as She had done with Jesus.

G.G. — *Mary led you to the heart of the Eternal Father. How did He reveal himself to you?*

G.F. — He revealed himself through his Son, Jesus crucified. It is while contemplating the wounds of Jesus that I grasped the infinite love of the Father for each one of us, especially for the most abject, among whom I belong.

G.G. — *Did you hear His voice?*

G.F. — Yes, but not as distinctly as I do now.

G.G. — *So now, how do you hear it?*

G.F. — I hear the voice of the Father like a voice which reprimands me with mercy, tenderness, being all the while firm as a father's would be.

G.G. — *What did He tell you?*

G.F. — As soon as He presented himself, He spoke to me of his Son. He spoke to me as a Father does to his child. Then I would address Him: "Eternal Father" or "Most Holy Father".

G.G. — *How did you come to the devotion to the Eternal Father?*

G.F. — By listening to Him attentively. I could see his great mercy in my life. And so, I began to know Him better and to serve and love Him better. THIS IS THE PURPOSE OF OUR EXISTENCE ON EARTH.

G.G. — *Have you anything else to add concerning your devotion to the Eternal Father?*

G.F. — Yes. In fact, His love for us exceeds the love He has for his Son, because WE NEED PURIFICATION WHILE HIS SON GAVE HIS LIFE TO PURIFY US. In the inmost part of his Heart as a Father, He loves us more in spite of our weaknesses and our sins. The more wretched we are, the nearer He is to us. The first step we take towards the Father, in spite of our sins, induces Him to shower us with His blessings. The least movement of repentance opens His Heart to his boundless mercy, for He is always ready to receive us and to forgive us.

G.G. — *Concretely how should we approach the Forgiveness of the Father?*

G.F. — By going to Jesus, the divine Priest who gave those who represent Him the power to remit sins and, thereby, to confirm us in the Forgiveness of the Father.

G.G. — *What does the Sacrament of Reconciliation bring to you?*

G.F. — The Sacrament of Reconciliation brings me a great peace of heart, of soul and of mind, because I feel the mercy of the Father, the love of Jesus and the peace of the Holy Spirit. This inner joy of the soul is given to us in the Sacrament of Reconciliation by the priest. How many depressions and anxieties would be avoided if we had recourse to this sacrament which often heals physical (i.e. alcoholism, drugs, etc.) and moral ills. We must not forget that the Virgin Mary asks us to have recourse frequently to all the sacraments.

G.G. — *We have spoken of your devotion to the Eternal Father, of his mercy, his forgiveness. But let us move on to something else. Has the Eternal Father spoken to you about Medjugorje?*

G.F. — No, the Eternal Father has not spoken to me directly about the apparitions of the Blessed Virgin at Medjugorje. The Holy Spirit is the one who inspires me the prayer I must make to ask with faith and trust that the apparitions of the Virgin Mary at Medjugorje be recognized.

G.G. — *You pray, therefore, that these apparitions be recognized?*

G.F. — Yes, I always pray to magnify the Father. So if the apparitions are recognized, this means GLORY for the Eternal Father, PRAISE for the Virgin Mary, Queen of Peace, and for us, grace and blessing.

G.G. — *What is the content of your prayer concerning the apparitions?*

G.F. — I speak to the Eternal Father about Mary, Queen of

Peace. I am convinced that this pleases Him, for everything that concerns the Mother of Jesus consoles Him. Then I ask Him to protect the visionaries, the Franciscan priests, the bishop, but especially that everyone may keep the requests and the messages of the Virgin Mary in their entirety so that all of these may be presented in their authenticity and in truth.

G.G. — *How does the Queen of Peace reveal herself to you?*

G.F. — To me, the QUEEN OF PEACE reveals herself nearer and nearer to me. *Mary is the INVISIBLE PRESENCE to the world to GIVE peace and the Holy Father John Paul II is the VISIBLE PRESENCE to ASK for that Peace.* It is through the apparitions of the Virgin Mary that the message of peace is brought to the earth. This message of peace will be carried throughout the world by the messenger of peace who is the Holy Father John Paul II.

G.G. — *We have spoken of what the Eternal Father was doing in your life. Can you make this more explicit?*

G.F. — Everything belongs to Him. This devotion gradually grew in my heart. I wanted to offer this heart of mine to Him as a shrine hoping to provide Him with a place of prayer that would become a dwelling place for Him on earth. This dream became reality in July 1960 with the permission of the bishop. Indeed, at that time, I set up a place for prayer in my rented home. This place of prayer was the first sanctuary dedicated to the Eternal Father.

G.G. — *What led you to dedicate your place for prayer to the Eternal Father?*

G.F. — It was because of the confidences of the Eternal Father that I wanted to offer Him this sanctuary. I knew that he would be consoled by the presence of Jesus and Mary. But it is a sanctuary on earth which is not made public.

G.G. — *Is there a public place dedicated to the Eternal Father?*

G.F. — No, the Father sadly told me one day: *There is nowhere on earth the least chapel dedicated to my name.*

G.G. — *What was your reaction?*

G.F. — I was sorry and I prayed that someday there might be a public sanctuary dedicated to his Name.

G.G. — *And then?*

G.F. — You know the answer to this better than I do. In May 1986, a chapel was dedicated to the glory of the Eternal Father. It is located in a hospital in Montreal. It was inaugurated on June 9, 1986.[1]

G.G. — *And so your wish and the Will of the Father have come true?*

G.F. — Yes, thanks to the Lord.

The Celestial Court

A.G. — *One day, you told me that you had asked the Eternal Father to send you an angel in addition to your Guardian Angel to help you in a difficult task. What did He answer?*

G.F. — *You have but to ask for help from the celestial court.* Surprised at this reply, I answered Him out loud: "Me?" And the Eternal Father replied: *Yes, because if I ask them to help you, they will obey me!*

A.G. — *Did you speak of this to your spiritual director?*

G.F. — Yes, and he told me: "My dear child, obey and especially do not hesitate to ask for help from the celestial court."

A.G. — *Do you believe we each have a guardian angel? Even the nonbelievers?*

G.F. — Yes, I believe it, because we are all children of God. And God entrusts us all, believers and nonbelievers, to our

---

1. This chapel is in a hospital in Laval City. The hospital, named "Cité de la Santé", is located at 1755, boulevard René Laennec, Laval (VIMONT), Quebec, Canada, H7M 3L9.

guardian angel so that he may protect us and keep us in the love of God.

A.G. — *What makes you say that?*

G.F. — Faith in what the Church teaches us, but also the experience of feeling that this guardian angel is close to me. This is difficult to describe, but it is certain that he is there. This is somewhat like a blind person being led by his guiding-dog; he does not see it, but he knows it is there. This presence is as evident as that.

A.G. — *Did you ever have a vision of your guardian angel?*

G.F. — No, but I feel his presence; he is always with us, whereas we must ask for the "Celestial Court" with faith.

A.G. — *Can you tell me what the celestial court has done for you?*

G.F. — It helps me at the spiritual level. It accompanies me in my prayer especially at the time of the Eucharist during the offering. At the moment of the consecration, it prostrates itself and adores the thrice holy God.

A.G. — *Do you have more than your Guardian Angel near you?*

G.F. — Yes, there are angels who watch over the Alliance; there are protecting angels who shield us from Satan.

A.G. — *Are there particular angels for the priests?*

G.F. — Yes, they have their guardian angel, as creatures of God. But they also have a very special angel for their priesthood, for at their consecration they are identified with Christ.

A.G. — *Can you give me an example that could be verified when the celestial court helped you?*

G.F. — When the Eternal Father asked me to kneel and to prostrate myself, I had the help of the celestial court. As you know, I have been an invalid for thirty-two years. This was an unwise move from the human point of view, but I made it in faith to obey the Eternal Father.

100

A.G. — *Do you have other examples?*

G.F. — Yes, you are a witness of experiences, even in the material domain, when the celestial court helps me. And certain tasks I fulfilled cannot be explained without a special help.

A.G. — *Georgette, we too often forget the angels and the celestial court, don't we?*

G.F. — Unfortunately, we have the tendency to forget the presence of our guardian angel and of the celestial court. Very often, the presence of our guardian angel is what protects us. We should invoke him and make him our confidant and our protector. It is comforting to know that he watches after us, that he sustains us in hardships and that he will accompany us when God calls us to Himself.

A.G. — *Have you anything else to add?*

G.F. — I advise you to have a very special devotion to Saint Michael the Archangel, and I would like the Church to resume the recitation of the prayer to Saint Michael the Archangel after Holy Mass. This would be a good protection for all the Church.

A.G. — *Do you make a link between the Eucharist and the celestial court?*

G.F. — Yes, during the Holy Eucharist, the Eternal Father sometimes allows me to see the whole multitude of angels and saints in a state of adoration around the altar! This is an invitation to the respect and to the dignity which must be given to the celebrant and to the participants. An attitude of respect is absolutely necessary before the Real Presence. We too often forget this and we hurt the Lord by these acts of disrespect.

A.G. — *What a profound remark, Georgette. Thank you.*

Conflicts with Satan and the Prostration

G.G. — *You remember, Father Armand and I had celebrated Holy Mass in your room when you were bedridden. You were to remain in bed according to the doctor's orders.*

G.F. — Yes. I was very weak but, nevertheless, the Eternal Father had asked me to make my act of thanksgiving with you in the little sanctuary.

G.G. — *Do you remember what happened during the act of thanksgiving?*

G.F. — Yes. We began to thank the Eternal Father. Suddenly, I could not pray anymore. Satan prevented me from doing so and I pronounced words beyond the control of my will.

G.G. — *Do you remember what you were saying?*

G.F. — Yes, but at that time, I did not realize all that was going on. There are some things I remember.

G.G. — *Does Satan attack you when you are alone?*

G.F. — Yes.

G.G. — *How?*

G.F. — He attacks me especially in my spiritual life. He persists in wanting to destroy me in my faith and in my trust. He makes me believe that all God is accomplishing in me is illusion, that I am damned for eternity. But he also attacks me when you are here. His aggressivity is greater because you are consecrated souls. When both of you are here, Satan is all the more furious and he has it out on me. God allows that, for by your priesthood, you can chase him away and protect me.

G.G. — *You said that Satan distorted your prayer. Can you give examples of that?*

G.F. — Yes. For example, he makes me say: "Thank you Jesus for allowing Satan to wander throughout the world for the good of souls" or "I hail myself Mary, Satan is with me" or again he curses the crown of thorns, the Alliance, the priests, the consecrated hands.

G.G. — *Sometimes, he attacks you physically?*

G.F. — Yes. You and your brother, you know that well. Sometimes, he tries to strangle me. You have already seen for yourselves the imprints of his fingers on my neck. But you have always succeeded in defending me and in chasing him away from me. He dreads priesthood, especially when the priest wears his stole.

G.G. — *How do these attacks end?*

G.F. — They stop almost everytime when you force Satan to bow his head and recite the "Hail, Mary" in full. He rages resorting to all his wiles against the title "Queen of Peace" which you invoke, but he can do nothing against Mary.

G.G. — *Tell me, since when do you have these attacks from Satan?*

G.F. — I have had them for a long time, but he is all the more furious since the Eternal Father asks me to offer Him my suffering and to pray for the authenticity of the apparitions at Medjugorje.

G.G. — *When did you hear about the apparitions of the Blessed Virgin in Medjugorje?*

G.F. — I heard about the apparitions of the Virgin Mary at Medjugorje from both of you about four years ago.

G.G. — *Can you tell me what the Lord asked you concerning these apparitions?*

G.F. — The Eternal Father asked me to pray more and to offer my suffering for the visionaries, for the priests of Medjugorje and in particular for the bishop of Mostar who bears a heavy responsibility.

G.G. — *Did He specify the name of the bishop?*

G.F. — Yes, He told me his name.

G.G. — *Now, well, something else about the prostration. Can you tell me again the date when the Lord explicitly asked you to prostrate yourself face down to the floor?*

G.F. — It was on Good Friday, April 5, 1985.

G.G. — *Why did He request this prostration?*

G.F. — The Eternal Father requested this prostration and He asked me to kiss the floor in reparation for the flagrant insults made to the Holy Eucharist. But he also requested it very clearly to help the bishop of Mostar, the visionaries and the Franciscans.

G.G. — *Why is this so difficult for you? And for how many years have you not knelt down?*

G.F. — For thirty-two years. I have been sick since the age of six. One day, when I was about forty, after a period of total immobility of my limbs, physicians decided to do surgery on the spinal column. There was no hope of success for this operation. The surgery was performed in the Notre Dame Hospital in Montreal. After the operation, doctors told me I would neither walk nor kneel again.

For a year and a half, I remained motionless on my bed. It was only after eighteen months that I began to walk again, but with very great difficulty.

G.G. — *Since this is so, were you frightened by the request the Eternal Father made to you that you prostrate yourself face down and kiss the floor?*

G.F. — No. I would have been afraid from the human point of view, because my chronic ill health did not allow me to kneel down and much less to prostrate myself. All movements of this type are forbidden by the doctor. Moreover, as I suffer from angina, this movement was an unwise one for me.

G.G. — *Yes, but you prostrated yourself?*

G.F. — Yes, but it was in sheer faith that I knelt and prostrated myself surrendering myself up totally to the Will of the Father. I had absolute trust in Him.

G.G. — *How did you hear this request to prostrate yourself?*

G.F. — It was in obedience to the inner voice that I knelt and prostrated myself.

G.G. — *Did you say any prayers at that moment?*

G.F. — Yes, certainly.

G.G. — *Which ones?*

G.F. — I was offering my suffering in union with that of Jesus and Mary for the salvation of souls, for the Holy Father John Paul II and for the universal Church. I offered it for Vicka who was to go through great trials, for the other visionaries, the priests of Medjugorje and the bishop of Mostar.

G.G. — *Does the Eternal Father still request this prostration?*

G.F. — Yes. He requests it on various occasions.

G.G. — *Can you give some examples?*

G.F. — For example, on the occasion of the Holy Father John Paul II's trips, for the success of the Synod, during the Holy Days.

G.G. — *Georgette, thank you.*

The Vow in the Night of Faith

On reading this testimony, some could believe that the life of the little servant of the Father is easy! We say NO to this. On this very day, on this feast of the Pentecost (May 18, 1986), Satan attacked the little servant of the Father saying to her:

"You have reached the peak of false prophets, I am happy about that; it is the result I have been waiting for for many years."

The greatest part of the life of the Father's little servant has been spent in darkness and today, especially now, she lives in a terrible night of faith. She experiences the agony of the soul, the heart and of the mind. It is, therefore, in sheer faith that she must go forward, for Satan tries to make her believe "with a sort of evidence" that all her life is a network of lies. She shares the agony of Jesus in the Garden of Gethsemane.

A few weeks ago, at the time when Jesus on the Cross was manifesting himself to her, He asked her with an appealing look:

"Come and follow me."

At that moment, Georgette answered Him: "Come and fetch me yourself for I am riveted to my bed by my suffering and I cannot move." And Jesus answered her:

"My hands are nailed to the cross by my consecrated souls, my priests. It is up to you to come to me..."

But the night still goes on...

Satan imitates the voice of Jesus or of Mary and speaks to her of her damnation if she does not give up this life of lies. These nights of darkness cannot be described in human words, for even death is a deliverance compared to these various states of the soul.

The little servant of the Father is nailed to the cross with an intensity of suffering, physical, moral and spiritual, which is ever increasing. Every day Jesus asks her to live in a state of immolation so that the Virgin Mary may triumph in this place (Medjugorje) where She has chosen to visit her children of earth. All the while we interrogated the little servant of the Eternal Father, Satan constantly made her believe she was damned for eternity. How often during the night, she heard him saying to her: "You are damned, and you are drawing these two priests along with you... They also believe in your life of lies, but someday they will curse the day they met you."

Satan's suggestions and all his subterfuges make a soul suffer more than a thousand deaths. But through this sea of darkness, where successive waves of the abyss brought to her by Satan seem to want to destroy her, God inspired his servant to make the vow of BELIEVING IN EVERYTHING GOD HAS ACCOMPLISHED IN HER. And it is to this vow that she must ever come back in the middle of her nights deprived of light. This is the lifebuoy which God has cast out for her. In spite of everything, she willingly bears all that the Father demands of her to become a witness of the apparitions of the Virgin Mary in Medjugorje. When you read the text of this vow, I ask you to pray for her so that the light of God may triumph over darkness.

Vow in the Night of Faith

In the presence of the Blessed Trinity,
In the presence of Mary Immaculate, Queen of Peace and Gate
of Heaven,
In the presence of the celestial court,
In the presence of Marie-Rose, my mother, and before my spiritual
director, Father Armand Girard, S.SS.A., and my spiritual
counsellor, Father Guy Girard, S.SS.A.,
I, Georgette Faniel, commit myself by a vow before the Precious
Blood of Jesus

To believe everything that God has accomplished in me,
which I do not understand,
but which I totally accept! through love!

I present this vow to Mary Immaculate, Queen of Peace, so
that I may die totally to myself, and become a witness to the
authenticity of the apparitions of the Virgin in Medjugorje.

I am making this vow in all freedom, to respond totally to the
Will of the Father for me.

This is also the vow I am making in order to identify myself
completely with Christ, priest and victim, to save souls, to renew
the heart of the priests of the entire Church until the end of time,
and for the glory of the Father. May this vow be a protection
for the Sovereign Pontiff John Paul II and for my spiritual sons,
Father Guy and Father Armand.

It is through the Power of the Holy Spirit and the Virgin Mary
that I shall fulfill this vow until the day when in His kindness the
Father will call me back to Himself. May God come to my aid!

In testimony whereof I have signed:

Georgette Faniel

Père Armand Girard s.ss.a.

Père Guy Girard ptre s.ss.a.

December 8, 1985, on the Feast of the Immaculate Conception

As we come to the end of this testimony which was not ever meant to be published, here are the questions we have asked ourselves:

Why choose to write this testimony which is more burdensome than silence?

Why would the Most Blessed Virgin Mary choose a poor Canadian who has always wished to remain secluded and keep the secret of the King in her heart?

Why would two Canadian priests who know the visionaries, the priests of Medjugorje well and what is happening in these places take the risk of being ridiculed and mocked by speaking of these mysterious bonds which link them to these events?

Why not remain hidden instead of taking this enormous burden on their shoulders?

Why not go on living with the certitude that prayer can advantageously take the place of this testimony?

ANSWER: Very simply because the road the Holy Spirit is showing us is the one which demands the most faith and the greatest surrender to the Most Holy and Adorable Will of the Eternal Father.

May 18, 1986, feast of Pentecost,

Father Armand Girard, S.SS.A.
Father Guy Girard, S.SS.A.

Appendix 3

To all those who have read this testimony.

Now that you have read this testimony, you are perhaps asking yourselves many questions: how could we have been so bold as to have written it. Please believe that we would not have wanted to speak of these events during the lifetime of the little servant of the Eternal Father, but, in good faith, we owed it to ourselves to write this testimony.

We have made this declaration in all freedom of mind having obtained the permission to say whatever we judged useful to testify to the authenticity of the apparitions of the Blessed Virgin at Medjugorje.

Many other facts show the love of God for his servant. We are remaining silent about these out of respect for what God is doing in her.

All that is written in this testimony is in accord with the facts; we pledge our priesthood to it.

We have sought but one thing: to be instruments docile to the inspirations of the Holy Spirit.

Father Armand Girard, S.SS.A.
Father Guy Girard, S.SS.A.

Testimony of Doctor Fayez Mishriki

I have known Georgette Faniel for three years. My first encounters with her were exchanges at the spiritual level. I am a physician, a general practitioner. At a time, when I was having difficult experiences in my life, I met this person who helped me rekindle my FAITH.

As a physician, I was able to notice phenomena in the life of Georgette which, according to me, modern science would find difficult to explain.

First, I must say that Georgette Faniel has an extremely long medical history, having undergone many surgeries for the spinal column, the liver, the intestines, the kidneys, etc. Several years ago, she became handicapped and confined to her room in her lodging, the result of a spinal column which has become ankylosed by arthrosis and of serious dizziness as well.

One very unusual phenomenon in Georgette's medical history is the appearance of a cutaneous lesion on her right side. In the course of a more careful examination, I was able to see that this cutaneous lesion has the perfect shape of the number two and is made up of many little red spots well vascularized individually. The lesion exists since the first of July 1982, the feast of the Precious Blood of Jesus and assumes a great spiritual significance in the life of Georgette Faniel. This number, VERY CLEARLY inlaid in her skin, is given to her as a testimony that Jesus makes the UNION OF TWO IN ONE IN SUFFERING.

Since October 1985, when her medical condition has become more serious, I have been able to follow the change in her more closely in my role as her doctor in attendance. She suffers from an accelerated chest angina with shortness of breath and fatigue. This angina is only partially controlled medically. Georgette suffers from a very sharp TRANSFIXING thoracic pain which comes when the Lord demands suffering from her for souls or for special events.

Georgette is able to discern between this pain and the one originating from her angina and she feels the pain disappear when she offers it to the Lord. And so, the physical, moral and spiritual afflictions of Georgette are always offered for the Church, the Holy Father, the consecrated souls, mankind and, for the last three years, the events of Medjugorje have been added to this list.

On the other hand, Georgette is very much affected in her general condition by nausea, lack of appetite and taste for food, and by sharp pains on her right side. In a strange way, in spite of a physical examination suspecting a hepatic and gastric illness, Georgette's pain goes ABSOLUTELY UNNOTICED IN ALL THE MEDICAL EXAMINATIONS she undergoes with difficulty in the hospital.

I wish to speak of a sign which is visible in Georgette and which assumes a spiritual significance and dimension. She often tells me that she has violent headaches, more severe on FRIDAYS. Inwardly, she knows that this is the crown of thorns of Jesus and confides this to me.

I admit having noticed on my own, at these moments, indentations (imprints, marks...) on Georgette's forehead, which disappear in normal times.

This is only a very brief testimony of the hidden and most mystical life of Georgette. It is important, even of prime importance, to say that all her suffering and afflictions are intimate, in union with those of Jesus and that they often are offerings for the souls in need of help. They are also VERY EXPLICITLY OFFERED FOR THE AUTHENTICITY OF THE APPARITIONS OF THE MOST BLESSED VIRGIN AT MEDJUGORJE.

Doctor Fayez Mishriki

A Witness of the Transfixion

Along with Fathers Guy and Armand Girard, S.SS.A., I was the witness of an absolutely unique phenomenon concerning Georgette Faniel. We were in the sanctuary making our act of thanksgiving, singing the SALVE REGINA and the hymn MIRTHA as well. During the MIRTHA hymn, I was surprised to hear Georgette singing it on a very high pitch, in one breath and in a strong and unfaltering voice. I noticed neither difficulty in breathing, no trouble in keeping her balance, nor any weariness. All this astonished me, given that, at the medical examination a few moments before, I had found Georgette much weakened and short of breath. Before that, she had had several thoracic discomforts of the ANGINA type.

After the hymn MIRTHA, what happened next cannot be explained in medical nor in scientific terms. Georgette suddenly felt a violent pain in the chest. This sudden and intense pain seized her so quickly that she was thrown back several centimeters. While she was clutching at her chest, I rushed to check her vital signs and much to my surprise neither her pulse nor her blood pressure had deviated from those of a normal condition. In her agony, Georgette had shown signs of difficulty in breathing.

As soon as she was seized by this pain, I was able to hear her thank God and continuously offer her suffering for the Church, for the priests and for Medjugorje so that the apparitions might be declared authentic. Georgette continued her offering and at times the pain resumed its initial intensity. Finally, it receded after about ten minutes. This pain appeared to be more intense than the agonizing one of a myocardial infarction.

Georgette explains to me that this pain is the agony of Jesus felt as if it were a dart piercing through her heart. This suffering, accepted and offered in union with that of Jesus, becomes redemptive as it frees a large number of souls from purgatory.

This phenomenon, which occurred in the presence of Fathers Guy and Armand Girard, was not new. It often takes place when Georgette attends a Holy Mass celebrated by the Fathers Girard, especially during the act of thanksgiving.

However, according to the Fathers Girard, this is the first time a doctor was present and can bear witness to this phenomenon which mystical theology defines as the transfixion of the heart.

I thank God for this unique grace and especially for having given me the opportunity to be a witness of it.

Doctor Fayez Mishriki

Mary, Queen of Peace.
Six years already. She appears.
What a visitation!

The Church of Medjugorje.
The irresistible love of Mary
draws people from all parts of the world.

Jozo Zovko

Tomislav Vlasić

Slavko Barbarić

Yvan Dugandzić

Tomislav Pervan

Petar Ljubicić

Vicka

Marija

Jakov

Ivan

Mirjana

Ivanka

Ecstasy 1981. The six visionaries listen to Mary.

Ecstasy 1985. Marija, Ivan, Jakov, Vicka.
"You are so beautiful, O Mary!"

Vicka, Jakov, Marija, Ivan.
"You are acclaimed by the angels."

Vicka, Ivan, Marija.
"You are the Queen of Peace!"

Hill of the apparitions.

Pilgrims kneel
at the place where
Mary set her feet.

Millions of pilgrims
climb the mountain
of the Cross (540 m — 1625 feet).

The mountain of the Cross.
Feast of the Exaltation of the Holy Cross
(September 14, 1985).

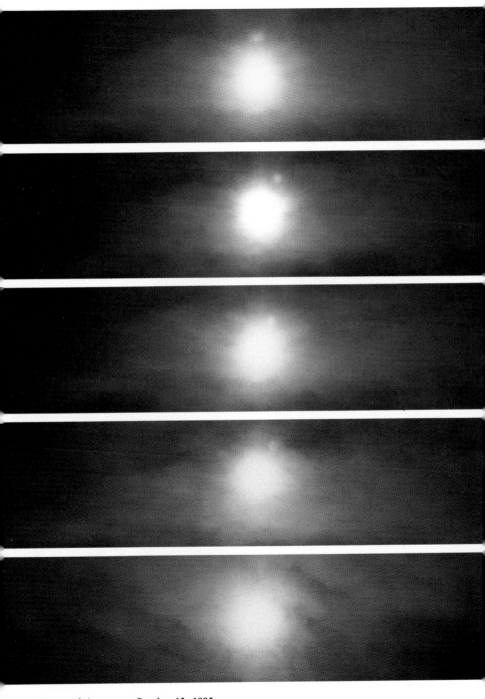

Dance of the sun on October 13, 1985.
Sequence of photos: Armand Girard.

Crowd at the
sacrament of reconciliation
at Medjugorje.

The Eucharist:
"The greatest
prayer on earth."

The young visionaries
in their everyday life
in Medjugorje.

Pictures of daily life in Medjugorje.

Jelena

Marijana

Those who "see with the heart".

Diana Basile,
healed in 1984 from
multiple sclerosis,
with Msgr. Zanić,
bishop of Mostar.

Agnès Heupel,
292nd person healed
at Medjugorje
(on 13-05-86).
Medical record
is being studied.

Father Armand Girard.
Georgette Faniel.
Father Guy Girard.
Pentecost 1982.

A spiritual bond exists between Medjugorje and Montreal.

Fraternal visit
of Father Pervan,
pastor of Medjugorje
(Montreal, October 8, 1986).

In the beautiful "chapel of the Eternal Father" rise prayers of offering for the triumph of Mary at Medjugorje ("Cité de la Santé" Hospital, Laval, June 6, 1986).

Father Laurentin and Doctor Ayoub at the opening of the double-themed conference: "Mary, Mother of the Redeemer" and "Scientific and medical studies on Medjugorje" (Notre Dame Hospital, Montreal, May 7, 1987).

Eternal Father,

I believe in You.
I love You.
I thank You.

With Mary,
I am confident
and I expect everything
from your love!

Pentecost 1987.
Beginning of a year
dedicated to Mary.

Part Four

Our Lady teaches us

Excerpts from the Thursday Messages

Introduction

Today many people already know about these messages. They
are primarily addressed to the parish of Medjugorje and then to
every person, family or parish who wishes to be led by Mary.
They are transmitted by telephone, radio, post, bulletins and are
distributed in many countries.

There are more and more communities which meditate them
in prayer groups every week, in the joyful expectation of the next
message. At first, not everyone understood the importance of
the message. Our Lady complained about this and even warned
that she would stop them. Now there is a much greater interest
in them. The messages reach a very large number of souls wishing
to let themselves be led by this eminent guide, who gives us a
clear call, offers us short counsels and profound recommendations. Today, after a few years, we detect Our Lady's intents and
her methods of teaching. She acts like a soft gentle rain which
penetrates earth more deeply than a quick passing shower. She
is motherly, gentle, patient and full of tact. She knows how we
are made. Following the example of her Son and of the patient
love of God, She repeats her messages ten, twenty times and,
if need be, two hundred times as she waits for us to open our

heart willingly and make decisions on our own. A story "about the wind and the sun who were competing as to which of the two would be the first to make a passerby remove his hat" seems very appropriate here. The wind was the first to set about to work; the more he blew, the more aggressive he was, the more the odds were against him, for the passerby, having felt the danger from the wind, held his hat down all the more securely with his hands and managed to thwart the intents of the wind. Then the sun entered into the game slowly, with perseverance. It beat down its rays harder and harder. Finally, the passerby decided to remove his hat to wipe off the sweat from his brow.

It seems that in Medjugorje the sun of kindness is doing precisely the same work. It is waiting for the greatest number of converts possible who, urged by this warmth of motherly love, will finally decide "to remove their hat" and bow willingly before their God and Savior so that Mary may obtain peace in the world. Mary is "Mater et Magistra" — "Mother and Master". To attend her school is most agreeable.

We have tried to group the messages according to themes to see better what are the "subjects" taught in her school. This will help us to shift the emphasis and lay it there where She insists the most to make the message obvious. In these messages, we clearly recognize the Woman who fights against the Serpent — Satan. Seeing her crying in the pains of childbirth, he does all he can to take the child about to be born from her. Now, She has taken refuge "in the desert", in the hearts of her most faithful children. She asks them to help her with prayer and sacrifice to realize the plan by which the earth will open up to swallow the lies of Satan, the lies he has used to poison the celestial stars and cast them down from the heaven of the Church.

Consequently, She shows the means we should take to win the victory over Satan with Her. These means are basically the main Gospel messages which numerous sons and daughters of the Church have now forgotten and even denied.

— Conversion, change of life.
— Prayer, fasting, penance.
— Faith in the Eternal Father who sends us Mary.
— Faith in the only Savior, the Son of God and Mary.

114

— Faith in the Holy Spirit who guides, strengthens and enlightens us.

— Faith in the Church, the sacraments, the Eucharist, Forgiveness (Reconciliation).

— Life in the love of God and neighbor.

— Faith in the existence of Satan who wanders throughout the world for the loss of souls. (Satan is neither a symbol, nor a negative force, but a fallen angel.)

— And so on...

She addresses her words to the priests, to the families, to the not so young, to everybody. She addresses especially her words to the parish of Medjugorje which She wishes to mold as a model parish serving as an example and a source of courage for all those who will go there as pilgrims. Meanwhile, we notice that the greater number of these messages deal with PRAYER. On June 12, 1986, She said: "You will understand why I remain so long with you. I want to teach you how to pray." Indeed, when we stop praying, faith dies in us, in our families, in our communities. The one who knows how to pray well knows how to live well. If we really knew how to pray, we would never need extraordinary interventions from God, for the Lord has told us that we can obtain everything through prayer. We receive and we find all we need to nourish our soul and our body: daily bread, the light of the Spirit, strength, comfort, joy and peace. These messages, as we have been able to observe, lead us to the depths of prayer, to the *prayer of the heart,* to a loving prayer. They speak to us of the experience of joy in prayer, of the glorification of God, of thanksgiving, of the experience of God in the Mass, of the adoration of the Blessed Sacrament and its effects, of prayer at the foot of the cross, of the meditation of the mysteries of the rosary, of a prayer prolonged and intensified by fasting to outwit Satan in his designs, of prayer to overcome temptations and to defeat Satan, of prayer which strengthens us in trials and through which we obtain healings, conversions and the love of neighbor.

At first, the children not knowing very well how to pray, on the advice of their grandmother, began by reciting the "Our Father" seven times; the Virgin Mary ratified this prayer. But we must not stop there and think that perhaps this is all She asks;

that would be a mistake. May those who will read these messages, particularly those on prayer, keep this in mind and let Mary lead them to the depths where we can catch large fish (abundant and substantial nourishment). Besides, let us allow ourselves to be challenged by the messages.

The Messages

Prayer

"Unite yourselves to my *prayer* for the parish so that His suffering may become bearable." (March 22, 1984)

"Today, I ask you to stop slandering and *pray* for unity in the parish." (April 12, 1984)

"Dear children, have compassion with me. *Pray, pray, pray.*" (April 19, 1984)

"I ask you not to let my heart shed tears of blood because of the souls who are losing themselves through sin. For that, dear children, *pray, pray, pray.*" (May 24, 1984)

"This evening, I would like to tell you to *pray* during this novena so that the Holy Spirit may come down on your families and on your parish. *Pray,* you will not be sorry that you did. God will grant you gifts for which you will magnify Him until the end of your life." (June 2, 1984)

"Tomorrow evening, *pray* for the Spirit of Truth, especially, you of the parish. *Pray* the Holy Spirit that He may give you the spirit of *prayer,* that you may *pray* more. I, your Mother, I am telling you: you *pray* too little." (June 9, 1984)

"*Pray, pray, pray.*" (June 21, 1984)

"Today, I would like to tell you to *pray* before your work and to end your work with *prayer.* If you do so, God will bless you and your work. These days, you are *praying* too little and working too much. *Pray* more. In *prayer* you will find rest." (July 5, 1984)

"During the coming days, Satan wants to thwart all my plans. *Pray* so that his scheme does not come about. I shall *pray* to my Son Jesus that He may give you the grace to see His victory over Satan's temptations." (July 12, 1984)

"Again today, I would like to invite you to persevere in *prayer* and penance. Especially, may the young people of this parish be more active in their *prayers*." (July 26, 1984)

"Today, I am happy and I thank you for your *prayers*. *Pray* more during these days for the conversion of sinners." (August 2, 1984)

"*Pray* because Satan is continually trying to thwart my plans. *Pray* with the heart and offer yourselves to Jesus in *prayer*." (August 11, 1984)

"I would like the people to *pray* with me these days. As much as possible, they must fast rigorously on Wednesdays and Fridays, *pray* at least the Rosary each day while meditating on the joyful, the sorrowful and the glorious mysteries." (August 14, 1984)

"*Pray, pray, pray!*" (August 23, 1984)

"These days especially, go to the mountain and *pray* at the foot of the cross. I need your *prayers*." (August 30, 1984)

"Without *prayer,* there is no peace. That is why I am telling you: dear children, *pray* at the foot of the cross for peace." (September 6, 1984)

"I continually need your *prayers*. You are asking yourselves, why so many *prayers*? Turn around, dear children, and you will see how sin has gained ground in this world. For that reason, *pray* that Jesus may triumph." (September 13, 1984)

"*Pray* and fast with the heart." (September 20, 1984)

"With your *prayers,* you have helped me carry out my plans. Pray yet more that they may be totally fulfilled. I ask the families

of the parish to recite the Rosary together in their family."
(September 27, 1984)

"Today, I would like to tell you that you often delight Me
with your *prayers*. But there are many of those in the parish who
do not *pray* and my heart is sad about that. For that reason, *pray*
so that I may bring all your sacrifices and your *prayers* to the
Lord." (October 4, 1984)

"Today, I am asking you to read the Holy Bible in your homes
every day and to place it in evidence so that you will remember
to read it and to *pray*." (October 18, 1984)

"*Pray* during this month. God has allowed Me to help you
each day with graces to protect you against evil. This month is
Mine. I give it to you. Only *pray,* and God will grant you the
graces you are asking. I will help you in that." (October 25, 1984)

"Today, I invite you to a renewal of *prayer* in your homes.
The work in the fields is over. Now, devote yourselves to *prayer.*
May *prayer* hold the first place in your families." (November 1,
1984)

"You are not aware of the messages God is sending you
through Me. He is giving you great graces and you do not
understand. *Pray* the Holy Spirit that He may enlighten you. If
you only knew how many graces God is giving you, you *would
pray* constantly." (November 8, 1984)

"You are a chosen people and the Lord has given you many
graces. You are not aware of every message I am giving you. Now,
I only wish to tell you this: *pray, pray, pray.* I don't know what
else to tell you, because I love you and I wish that in *prayer,* you
may come to know my love and the love of God." (November
15, 1984)

"You do not listen with love to the words I give you. Be aware,
my beloved, that I am your Mother and that I have come on earth
to teach you how to listen with love, how to *pray* with love."
(November 29, 1984)

"During these coming days, I invite you to family *prayer*...

This Christmas will be unforgettable for you provided you accept the messages I give you." (December 6, 1984)

"May this week be a week of *thanksgiving* for all the graces God has given you." (January 3, 1985)

"My dear children, Satan is so powerful and he uses all his power to obstruct my plans for you. *Pray, pray* constantly, and do not stop doing so for one moment. I too, will *pray* my Son so that all my plans for you may be fulfilled. Be patient and perseverant in your *prayers*! Do not let yourselves to be discouraged by Satan. He is very powerful in this world. Be cautious!" (January 14, 1985)

"These days, you were able to savor the sweetness of God through the renewal which has taken place in your parish. Satan wants to work yet harder to take away the joy that is in each one of you. Through *prayer*, you can disarm him completely and assure your happiness." (January 24, 1985)

"During these days, Satan manifests himself in a particular way in this parish. *Pray*, dear children, that God's plans may be carried out and that all the action of Satan may turn out to be for the glory of God." (February 7, 1985)

"Each family must make the family *prayer* and read the Bible." (February 14, 1985)

"Day after day, I have called you to a renewal and to *prayer* in your parish, but you do not accept that. Today, I am inviting you for the last time. This is Lent and you, in the parish, during this season, can be moved for the sake of my love to respond to my call." (February 21, 1985)

"I invite you to renew *prayer* in your families. Dear children, encourage the very young to *pray* and to go to Holy Mass." (March 7, 1985)

"Today, I wish to remind you: *Pray, pray, pray!* In *prayer* you will come to know the greatest joy and the means of resolving all situations which seem to be without solutions. Thank you for progressing in *prayer*. Every individual is dear to my heart and

I thank all those among you who have rekindled *prayer* in your families." (March 28, 1985)

"Today, I want to tell each one in the parish to *pray* in a special way to receive the light of the Holy Spirit." (April 11, 1985)

"Say all your *prayers* so that the hearts of sinners may be opened. I want this, God wants this through Me." (April 18, 1985)

"Today, I am calling you to *prayer* in the heart and not to one of routine. Some are coming but do not wish to go further in *prayer*. For this reason, I beg you as a Mother, *pray* so that *prayer* may prevail in your hearts at every moment." (May 2, 1985)

"No, you don't know how many graces God is granting you! You don't want to go further during these days when the Holy Spirit is acting in a special way. Your hearts are turned towards the things of this world and you are preoccupied by them. Turn your hearts to *prayer* again and ask that the Holy Spirit may be poured forth in you." (May 9, 1985)

"I am calling you to a more active *prayer* and to a greater participation in the Mass. I want the Mass to be an experience of God for you. I especially want to say to the young people: be open to the Holy Spirit because God wants to draw you to Himself in these times when Satan is active." (May 16, 1985)

"I invite you again to the *prayer* of the heart. Dear children, may *prayer* be your daily nourishment, especially when the work in the fields consumes all your energy and you cannot *pray* with your heart. *Pray* and, in this way, you will overcome all fatigue. *Prayer* will be your joy and your rest." (May 30, 1985)

"I invite you, members of the parish, to *pray* more until the anniversary of the apparitions. May your *prayer* become the sign of your surrender to God." (June 13, 1985)

"I urge you to invite everbody to the *prayer* of the rosary. With the rosary, you will overcome all the difficulties that Satan wants to inflict on the Catholic Church. You, priests, *pray* the rosary, devote some time to the Rosary." (June 25, 1985)

"I love the parish and I protect it with my mantle from the wiles of Satan. *Pray* that Satan may flee from this parish and from every individual who comes to this parish. This way, you will be able to hear every call from God and to respond to it by your life." (July 11, 1985)

"Satan has taken over a part of the plan and wants to make it his own. *Pray* that he might not succeed because I want you for myself so I can offer you to God." (August 1, 1985)

"Today, I invite you, and especially now, to begin already the combat against Satan with *prayers.* Arm yourselves against Satan and with the Rosary in your hand you will triumph." (August 8, 1985)

"Today, I would like to tell you that the Lord wants to put you through a test, but you can overcome with *prayer.* God puts you through a test in your everyday work. Now, pray that you might overcome every trial." (August 22, 1985)

"I invite you to *prayer,* especially now when Satan wants to use the harvests of your vineyards. *Pray* that he might not succeed in carrying out his plan." (August 29, 1985)

"Today, I thank you for all your *prayers. Pray* continuously and even more so that Satan may go away from this place. Dear children, Satan's plan has fallen through. *Pray* that God's plan may be realized in this parish." (September 5, 1985)

"I want to tell you that, during these days, the Cross must be put at the center of your life. *Pray* especially before the Cross, from which flow great graces. Now, in your homes, make a special consecration to the Cross." (September 12, 1985)

"I thank you for all the *prayers.*" (September 26, 1985)

"I wish to tell you to be grateful towards the Lord for every grace He has given you. Thank the Lord for all the fruits and praise Him. Dear children, learn to be thankful in little things and then you will be able to be thankful in great things." (October 3, 1985)

"*Pray* and love." (November 7, 1985)

"I, your Mother, I love you. I wish to urge you to *prayer*. Dear children, I never grow weary, I call you even if you are far from my heart." (November 14, 1985)

"During the summer, you say you have much work to do. Now that there is no work to do in the fields, work on yourselves. Come to Mass, as this time is given for you. Dear children, there are so many who come regularly in spite of bad weather, for they love Me and they want to show Me their love in a special way. I ask you to show Me your love by coming to Mass. The Lord will reward you generously." (November 21, 1985)

"I beg you, dear children, enter into *prayer* consciously, and it is in *prayer* that you will know the majesty of God." (November 28, 1985)

"I invite you to prepare yourselves for the feast of Christmas by penance, *prayer* and acts of love." (December 5, 1985)

"On Christmas, I invite you to praise Jesus together with Me. On that day, I give Him to you in a special way and I invite you to celebrate Jesus and his birth with Me. Dear children, on that day, *pray* more. And think more about Jesus." (December 12, 1985)

"I invite you to help Jesus with your *prayers* for the realization of all the plans He has already begun to carry out here." (January 9, 1986)

"Today also, I invite you to *prayer*; I need your *prayers* so that God may be glorified through all of you." (January 16, 1986)

"I invite you again to the *prayer* of the heart. If you *pray* with the heart, dear children, the ice-cold hearts of your brothers will melt and every barrier will disappear. Conversion will be easy for all those who want it. This is a favor which you must beg for your neighbor." (January 23, 1986)

122

"Today, I invite you all to *pray* for the realization of God's plans and His wishes for you. Help others to convert themselves, especially all those who come to Medjugorje... I invite you to *pray* that you may become witnesses of my presence." (January 30, 1986)

"I offer great graces to those who *pray* with the heart." (February 6, 1986)

"The second message for Lenten days is that you renew your *prayer* before the Cross. Dear children, I offer you special graces and Jesus offers you special gifts from the Cross. Accept them and live them. Meditate on the passion of Jesus and unite yourselves to Jesus in your daily life." (February 20, 1986)

"Today again, I call you to open yourselves more to God so that He may work through you. Inasmuch as you open yourselves to him, so will you receive fruits. I wish to invite you again to *prayer*." (March 6, 1986)

"Today, I invite you to be more active in *prayer*. You wish to live everything I am telling you but you don't succeed because you don't *pray*. Dear children, I beg you, open your hearts and begin to *pray*. *Prayer* will be a delight for you if you begin. *Prayer* will not be boring, for you will *pray* out of pure joy." (March 20, 1986)

"I wish to invite you to live the Holy Mass. There are many among you who have felt the beauty of the Mass, but there are others who come unwillingly. I have chosen you, dear children, but Jesus gives his graces in Holy Mass. Because of that, live the Holy Mass consciously. May each attendance to Mass be full of joy for you. Come with love and accept the Holy Mass." (April 3, 1986)

"I invite you, dear children, to *pray* for the gifts of the Holy Spirit which you need now in order that you may testify to my presence here, to everything I am giving you." (April 17, 1986)

"Today, I am inviting you to *pray*. Dear children, you forget that you are all important. The elderly especially are important in the family. Incite them to *pray*... I beg you to begin to change through *prayer* and you will know what you must do." (April 24, 1986)

"I beg you to begin to change your life within the family. May the family be a flower of harmony I may offer to Jesus. Dear children, may each family be active in *prayer* so that someday we may also see fruits in the family. Then only I will offer you all as petals to Jesus like the realization of the plans of God." (May 1, 1986)

"Today, I urge you to begin to *pray* the Rosary with a living faith. Then only, will I be able to help you. Dear children, you want to receive graces, but you do not *pray*. I cannot help you if you do not want to start moving. Dear children, I invite you to *pray* the Rosary so that it may be a commitment you will fulfill with joy. Thus, you will understand why I am visiting you for such a long time. I want to teach you to *pray*." (June 12, 1986)

"These days, the Lord has allowed me to obtain more graces for you. For this reason, I invite you again to *pray*. *Pray* constantly; then, I will be able to give you the joy that the Lord gives me." (June 19, 1986)

"There are people who, by their indifference, destroy peace and *prayer*. I invite you to witness and to help by your life to keep this oasis intact." (June 26, 1986)

"Today, I invite you all to *prayer*. Without *prayer,* dear children, you can neither perceive God, nor me, nor the graces I give you. Here is what I am inviting you to do: let the beginning and the end of your day be always a *prayer*... May *prayer* always hold the first place for you." (July 3, 1986)

"You know what I have promised you: an oasis of peace but you ignore that around every oasis, there is a desert where Satan keeps watch and wants to try each one of you. Dear children, it is only through *prayer* that you may overcome the influence of Satan." (August 7, 1986)

"May your *prayer* be a joyful encounter with the Lord. I cannot guide you there unless you yourself experience joy in *prayer*. I want to lead you to a greater depth in *prayer* from day

124

to day, but I cannot force you to do that." (August 14, 1986)

"From day to day, I pray the Lord to help you understand the love I show you. For this, dear children, *pray, pray, pray.*" (August 21, 1986)

"I invite you to be an example for others in every way, especially in *prayer* and in witnessing. Dear children, without you I cannot help the world. I wish you to cooperate with Me in everything, even in the least little actions. For this, dear children, help Me; may your *prayer* be a *prayer* of the heart and may you surrender yourselves totally to Me. On this condition, I will be able to teach you and guide you on this journey which I have begun with you." (August 28, 1986)

"Today, again, I invite you to *prayer* and fasting. Know, dear children, that with your help I can do everything and prevent Satan from misleading you and force him to go away from this place... I invite you to make of your day nothing but *prayer* and total surrender to God." (September 4, 1986)

"*Pray* that you may be able to accept illness and suffering with love as Jesus did. Only then will I be able to grant you with joy the graces and healings Jesus allows Me to give you." (September 11, 1986)

"Therefore, I call you through *prayer* and your life to help to destroy all that is evil in men and to discern the lies that Satan uses to lose souls. *Pray* so that Truth may triumph in your hearts." (September 25, 1986)

"Today, again, I call you to *prayer*. You, dear children, you cannot understand the value of *prayer* if you don't say with yourselves that now is the time to *pray*; nothing else is important; now no one else is important to Me except God. Dear children, dedicate yourselves to *prayer* with a special love; and so God will be able to give you graces." (October 2, 1986)

"This is why, dear children, I am inviting you to *prayer* and to a total surrender to God because Satan wishes to win you over in everyday affairs and take the first place in your life. Therefore, dear children, *pray* unceasingly." (October 16, 1986)

125

"Today, again, I call you to *prayer*; I invite you more particularly, dear children, to *pray* for peace. Without your *prayers*, dear children, I cannot help you realize the messages that the Lord has allowed me to give you. Therefore, dear children, *pray* to know in *prayer* the peace the Lord gives you." (October 23, 1986)

"Today, I want to invite you to *pray* everyday for the souls in purgatory. Every soul needs *prayers* and graces to reach God and to develop the love of God... Therefore, dear children, *pray* without stopping in order to be able to help yourselves as well as others to whom your *prayers* will bring joy." (November 6, 1986)

"Today also, I invite you to *pray* with all your heart and to change your life from day to day. I especially invite you, dear children, to begin a life of holiness with your *prayers* and sacrifices... For this reason, dear children, *pray* and, from day to day, change your life in order to be holy." (November 13, 1986)

"*Pray,* dear children, for only then will you be able to know all the evil that is in you and hand it over to the Lord so that He may purify your hearts completely. *Pray* constantly and purify your hearts in penance and fasting." (December 4, 1986)

"I invite you to *pray* especially at this time so that you may experience the joy of meeting the newborn Jesus... Therefore, dear children, *pray* and abandon yourselves completely to me." (December 11, 1986)

"Today, I want to invite you again to *prayer.* When you *pray,* you are much more beautiful, like the flowers which, after the snows, show all their beauty and colors become indescribable. Similarly, dear children, after *prayer* you also display to a greater degree before God all that is beautiful in you to please Him. Therefore, dear children, *pray* and open your inner self to the Lord so that He may make of you harmonious and beautiful flowers for Paradise." (December 18, 1986)

"Therefore, dear children, *pray* without stopping and put all the messages I give you into practice, for I am doing this with great love for God and for you. (January 1, 1987)

126

"Especially, dear children, thank you for all the sacrifices and the *prayers* you have offered Me." (January 8, 1987)

"Therefore, dear children, *pray* so that you may know through *prayer* God's plan on each of you." (January 25, 1987)

"*Pray* and you will know in *prayer* the new way of joy. Joy will reveal itself in your hearts; and so, you will be the joyful witnesses of what my Son and I expect from each one of you." (February 25, 1987)

"I invite you all to *prayer*. You know, dear children, that God gives special graces in *prayer*. Therefore, seek and *pray* to be able to understand all I am giving you in this place. I invite you to the *prayer* of the heart. You know that without *prayer* you cannot understand all that God is planning through each one of you. *Pray* for that. I wish that God's plan may be fulfilled in each one of you and that everything He has put in your hearts may grow. Therefore, *pray* that God's blessing may protect you from all the evil that is threatening you." (April 25, 1987)

"Tonight, when Our Lady came... She immediately *prayed* over all of us for a certain length of time, and we asked for a blessing... We *prayed* to her for the needs of each one of us who were here tonight." (Reported by Marija on June 24, 1987)

"Today again, I wish to invite you all to *prayer,* let *prayer* be LIFE for you. Dear children, devote some time to Jesus alone, and He will give you all you seek. He will fully reveal himself to you... Satan is strong and he lies in wait to tempt each one of you. *Pray* so that he will be able neither to harm you nor to block you on the way of holiness. From day to day, grow as much as possible closer to God in *prayer*." (September 25, 1987)

"*Pray,* for in *prayer,* each one of you will be able to reach perfect love." (October 25, 1987)

"Dear children, I wish everything God has planned for this parish may come true, but if you don't *pray,* you cannot discover my love and the plan God has for this parish and for each one of you. *Pray* that Satan may not entice you with his pride and his deceitful power." (November 25, 1987)

"I want each of you to open his heart to Jesus and I will give Him to you with love. Dear children, I want Him to change you, to teach you and to protect you. Today I am *praying* for each one of you in a special way and I am presenting you to God so that He may reveal himself to you. I call you to a sincere *prayer* of the heart, so that each of your *prayers* may be an encounter with God. In your work, in your daily life, let God have the first place." (December 25, 1987)

"I want to call you to *prayer* and to a total surrender to God... If you *pray,* Satan cannot harm you, for you are children of God, and He is the one watching over you. *Pray*; and you may always keep the Rosary in your hands as a sign that you belong to Me, a sign against Satan." (February 25, 1988)

"He allows Me to be with you to teach you and to help you find the way of Peace. But you cannot find this way if you do not *pray*... *PRAY* so that your *prayer* and your surrender to God may become a sign." (March 25, 1988)

"Be aware that the church is God's palace, a place where I gather you and want to show you the way leading to God. Come and *pray*... Believe, and *pray* that the Father may increase your faith; then you may ask for what you need." (April 25, 1988)

"*Pray* together so that the Devil may not sway you as the wind does the reed... *Pray* constantly so that the Devil may not take advantage of you. *Pray* so that you may be able to understand that you belong to Me." (May 25, 1988)

The Young People

"Again today, I would like to invite you to persevere in prayer and penance. Especially, may the *young people* of this parish be more active in their prayers." (July 26, 1984)

"Pray, pray, pray. I also appeal to the people, especially to the *young people* to maintain order in the church during Mass." (August 23, 1984)

"Today, I thank you for all your prayers. Pray continuously

and even more so that Satan may go far away from this place. Dear children, Satan's plan has fallen through. Pray that God's plan be realized in this parish. I especially thank the *young people* for the sacrifices they have offered." (September 5, 1985)

"Today, I would like to invite you to live the messages to the parish; especially, I want to call the *young people* of this parish which is so dear to Me. Dear children, if you live the messages, you will foster the growth of the seeds of holiness. As a Mother, I call all of you to holiness so that you may radiate to others. You are like a mirror for the people." (October 10, 1985)

"I want to thank you all for what you have done for Me, especially the *young people*. I beg you, dear children, enter into prayer consciously and it is in prayer that you will know the majesty of God." (November 28, 1985)

The Parish of Medjugorje

"I have chosen this *parish* in a special way and I want to guide it. I am keeping it in love and I would like everyone to be Mine. I thank you for being here this evening. I would like you to be always more and more numerous with my Son and Myself. Every Thursday, I will give you a special message." (March 1, 1984)

"I thank you for having answered my call. Dear children, you of the *parish,* convert yourselves. This is my second wish. And so, all those who will come here will be able to convert themselves." (March 8, 1984)

"This evening, I invite you in a special way, during this Lent, to venerate the wounds of my Son, which He bored for the sins of this *parish*. Unite yourselves to my prayers for the *parish* so that His suffering may become bearable." (March 22, 1984)

"Today, I ask you to stop slandering and pray for the unity of the *parish,* because my Son and I have a special plan for this *parish*." (April 12, 1984)

"I do not want to force anyone to do anything he does not feel nor wish, even though I had special messages for the *parish*

129

to rekindle the faith of every believer. But very few have accepted the Thursday messages. At first, they were quite numerous, but this has become as a habit for them. And now, a few ask for the messages only out of curiosity, and not out of faith in and devotion to my Son and Me.'' (April 30, 1984)

"I speak to you and I intend to speak to you again. Only listen to my instructions.'' (May 10, 1984)

"Today, I have much joy because several among you want to devote themselves to Me. I thank you! You are not making a mistake. My Son, Jesus Christ, wants to bestow special graces on you through Me. My Son is rejoiced by your surrender.'' (May 17, 1984)

"I have already told you that I have chosen you in a special way such as you are. I, the Mother, I love you all. And at any moment, when things are difficult, do not fear. For I love you even when you are far away from Me and my Son. I ask you not to let my heart shed tears of blood because of the souls who are losing themselves through sin.'' (May 24, 1984)

"Today, also, I would like to thank you for all your sacrifices, and I address very special thanks to those who have become dear to my heart and who willingly come here. There are some *parishioners* who do not listen to my messages, but because of those who, in a special way, are close to my heart, because of them, I give messages to the *parish*. And I will continue to give some because I love you and I wish you to spread my messages with your heart.'' (January 10, 1985)

"These days, Satan is deviously fighting against this *parish,* and you, dear children, have fallen asleep in prayer and few are those who go to Mass. Persevere in these days of trials.'' (January 17, 1985)

"These days, you were able to savor the sweetness of God through the renewal which has taken place in your *parish*. Satan wants to work yet harder to take away the joy that is in each one of you. Through prayer, you can disarm him completely and assure your happiness.'' (January 24, 1985)

130

"During these days, Satan manifests himself in a particular way in this *parish*. Pray, dear children, that God's plans may be carried out and that all the action of Satan may turn out to be for the glory of God." (February 7, 1985)

"Today is the day I give the messages for the *parish,* but not all in the *parish* accept the messages and put them into practice. I am sad, and, dear children, I would like you to listen to Me and to live my messages. Each family must make the family prayer and read the Bible." (February 14, 1985)

"Day after day, I have called you to a renewal and to prayer in your *parish,* but you do not accept that. Today, I am inviting you for the last time. This is Lent, and you, in the *parish,* during this season, can be moved for the sake of my love to respond to my call. If you do not do that, I do not wish to give you any more messages. God is allowing Me to do that." (February 21, 1985)

"Today, I am inviting you to live these words during this week: 'I love God'. Dear children, you will obtain everything through Love, and even what you believe to be impossible. God wants this *parish* to belong to Him completely. I also want this to be so." (February 28, 1985)

"You have all experienced light and darkness in your life. God gives the knowledge of good and evil to everyone. I urge you to reflect on the Light you must give to all those who are in darkness. From day to day, people who are in darkness come to your homes. Dear children, give them the light." (March 14, 1985)

"I want to give you the messages and, therefore, today also, I urge you to live and to accept my messages. Dear children, I love you; and, in a special way, I have chosen this *parish* which is dearer to Me than others where I have gladly been when the Almighty sent Me. Therefore, I urge you: accept Me, dear children, for the sake of your well-being. Listen to my messages and put them into practice." (March 21, 1985)

"I thank you because, in your hearts, you think more of the

glory of God. Today, I wanted to stop giving the messages because some individuals do not accept them. The *parish* has responded and I want to continue giving you the messages as was never done before in history since the beginning of the world." (April 4, 1985)

"You, the *parishioners,* have a large and heavy cross. But do not be afraid to carry it. My Son is there to help you." (April 5, 1985)

"Today, I want to tell each one in the *parish* to pray in a special way to receive the light of the Holy Spirit. From this moment, God wants to put the *parish* to the test in a special way in order to strengthen it in faith." (April 11, 1985)

"Today, I thank you for all the openness of your hearts. I am overwhelmed for each heart that opens itself to God, especially in the *parish*. Rejoice with Me! Say all your prayers so that the heart of sinners may be opened. I want this, God wants this through Me." (April 18, 1985)

"I invite you again to the prayer of the heart. Dear children, may prayer be your daily nourishment, especially when the work in the fields consumes all your energy and you cannot pray with your heart. Pray and, in this way, you will overcome all fatigue. Prayer will be your joy and your rest." (May 30, 1985)

"During these coming days, people of all nationalities will come to the *parish*. And now, I invite you to love. Love first of all the members of your own family, then you will be able to accept and love all those who come." (June 6, 1985)

"I invite you, members of the *parish,* to pray more until the anniversary of the apparitions. May your prayer become the sign of your surrender to God. Dear children, I know that you are tired. But you don't know how to abandon yourselves to Me. Abandon yourselves totally to Me these days." (June 13, 1985)

"I love this *parish* and I protect it with my mantle from all the wiles of Satan. Pray that Satan may flee away from the *parish* and from every individual who comes to the *parish*. This way, you will be able to hear every call from God and respond to it with your life." (July 11, 1985)

"I want to tell you that I have chosen this *parish* and that I keep it in my hands like a little flower that does not want to die. I invite you to surrender yourselves to Me so that I may offer you, pure and without sin, to God. Satan has taken over a part of the plan and wants to make it his own. Pray that he might not succeed because I want you for Myself so I can offer you to God." (August 1, 1985)

"I invite you to prayer, especially now when Satan wants to use the harvests of your vineyards. Pray that he might not succeed in carrying out his plan." (August 29, 1985)

"Today, I thank you for all your prayers. Pray continuously and even more so that Satan may go away, far from this place. Dear children, Satan's plan has fallen through. Pray that God's plan may be realized in this *parish*. I especially thank the young people for the sacrifices they have offered." (September 5, 1985)

"I thank you for all your prayers and sacrifices. I want to tell you, dear children, to live again the messages I give you. Especially revive fasting, because with fasting, you will rejoice Me and obtain that the Lord's project for Medjugorje may be entirely realized." (September 26, 1985)

"Today, I would like to invite you to live the messages of the *parish,* especially I would like to call the young people of this *parish* which is so dear to Me. Dear children, if you live the messages, you will foster the growth of the seeds of holiness. As a Mother, I call all of you to holiness so that you may radiate it on others. You are like a mirror for the people." (October 10, 1985)

"There is a time for every thing. Today, I invite you to begin to work on your hearts. All the work in the fields is completed. You find time to clean up the most forsaken places, but you leave your hearts aside. Be more industrious and, with love, clean every corner of your hearts." (October 17, 1985)

"I invite you to the love of your neighbors, especially those who hurt you. Then you will be able to judge the intentions of hearts with love. Pray and love, dear children. With the power of love, you will be able to accomplish things which appear impossible to you." (November 7, 1985)

"This time is there especially for you of this *parish*. During the summer, you say you have much work to do. Now that there is no work in the fields, work on yourselves. Come to Mass, as this time is given for you. Dear children, there are so many who come regularly in spite of bad weather, for they love Me and they want to show Me their love in a special way. I ask you to show Me your love by coming to Mass. The Lord will reward you generously." (November 21, 1985)

"I invite you to help Jesus with your prayers for the realization of all the plans He has already begun to carry out here. Offer your sacrifices to Jesus so that He may fulfill all He has planned and so that Satan may not be able to do anything." (January 9, 1986)

"This *parish* which I chose is special. It stands out from the others. This is the reason why I offer great graces to all those who pray with the heart. Dear children, I am giving you my messages first of all for the *parishioners* and, then, for all the others. You must be the first to accept them and the others are then invited to receive them. You are responsible for these before my Son Jesus and Myself." (February 6, 1986)

"Today, I invite you to live the love for God and for your neighbor. Without love, dear children, you can do nothing. Here is why I invite you to live in mutual love. Only then will you be able to love and to accept Me and all those around you, all those who come to your *parish*. All will perceive my love through you. This is the reason why I beg you, dear children, beginning today, start to love with a burning love, the love with which I love you." (May 29, 1986)

"God allowed Me to bring about with Him this oasis of peace. I am going to invite you to keep it intact. There are people who, by their indifference, destroy peace and prayer. I invite you to witness and to help by your life to keep this oasis intact." (June 26, 1986)

"Today, again, I invite you to prayer and fasting. Know, dear children, that with your help I can do everything and prevent Satan from misleading you and force him to go away from this place. Dear children, Satan lies in wait for each one of you. He especially wants to sow the seeds of suspicion in each of you in everyday things. Therefore, I invite you to make your day nothing but prayer and total surrender to God." (September 4, 1986)

"Dear children, I wish everything God has planned for this *parish* may come true, but if you do not pray, you cannot discover my love and the plan God has for this *parish* and for each one of you." (November 25, 1987)

Conversion and Change of One's Life

"Dear children, you of the parish, *convert* yourselves." (March 8, 1984)

"Today, I am happy and I thank you for your prayers. Pray more these days for the *conversion* of sinners." (August 2, 1984)

"Day after day, I have called you to a renewal and to prayer in your parish but you do not accept that. Today, I am inviting you for the last time. This is Lent and you, in the parish, during this season, can be moved for the sake of my love to respond to my call. If you do not do that, I do not wish to give you any more messages. God allows Me to do this." (February 21, 1985)

"Today, I thank you for the openness of your hearts. I am overwhelmed with joy for each heart that opens itself to God, especially in the parish. Rejoice with Me. Say all your prayers so that the hearts of sinners may be opened. I want this, God wants this through Me." (April 18, 1985)

"No, you don't know how many graces God is granting you! You do not want to go further these days when the Holy Spirit is acting in a special way. Your hearts are turned towards the things of this world and you are preoccupied with them. Turn your hearts to prayer again and ask that the Holy Spirit be poured upon you." (May 9, 1985)

"These days, I invite you especially to open your hearts to the Holy Spirit who is working through you. Open your hearts and offer your lives to Jesus that He may work in your hearts and strengthen you in faith." (May 23, 1985)

"For this feast, I want to tell you to open your hearts to the Lord of all hearts. Give Me all your thoughts and your problems. I want to comfort you in your trials. I would like to fill you with the peace, the joy and the love of God." (June 20, 1985)

"I, your Mother, I love you. I wish to urge you to prayer. Dear children, I never grow weary; I call you even if you are far away from my heart. I am a Mother; I suffer for everyone of my children who goes astray, but I forgive them easily and I rejoice when one of my children comes back to Me." (November 14, 1985)

"I invite you again to the prayer of the heart. If you pray with the heart, dear children, the ice-cold hearts of your brothers will melt and every barrier will disappear. *Conversion* will be easy for all those who want it. This is a favor which you must beg for your neighbor." (January 23, 1986)

"Today, I invite you all to pray for the realization of God's plans and His wishes for you. Help others to *convert* themselves, especially all those who come to Medjugorje. Dear children, do not let Satan become the master of your hearts because, in this case, you will become the image of Satan and not of Me. I invite you to pray so that you may be witnesses of my presence. Without you, the Lord cannot realize all He wishes. The Lord has given you all a free will and you may dispose of it as you wish." (January 30, 1986)

"This Lent is a special incentive for you to change your life. Begin right now. Turn off your television sets and renounce the various things which are of no use to you. Dear children, I invite you to a personal *conversion*. This is the time for you." (February 13, 1986)

136

"Today, I am inviting you to pray. Dear children, you forget that you are all important. The elderly especially are important in the family. Incite them to pray. May all the young people be a living example for the others and may they be a witness to Jesus. Dear children, I beg you to begin to change through prayer and you will know what you must do." (April 24, 1986)

"I beg you to begin to change your life within the family. May your family be a flower of harmony that I may offer to Jesus. Dear children, may every family be active in prayer so that someday we may also see its fruits. Then, I will offer you all as petals to Jesus for the realization of the plans of God." (May 1, 1986)

"Today, I invite you to give Me your heart that I may change it and make it similar to Mine. You ask yourselves, dear children, why you cannot comply with what I request from you. You are not able to do so because you have not given Me your heart so that I may change it. You say you will but you don't do it. I invite you to do everything I ask you. Then, I shall be with you." (May 15, 1986)

"For this reason, dear children, pray and, from day to day, change your life in order to be holy." (November 13, 1986)

"Therefore, dear children, today, turn your mind again to God." (November 27, 1986)

"Pray, dear children, for only then will you be able to know all the evil that is in you and hand it over to the Lord so that He may purify your hearts completely." (December 4, 1986)

"Starting from today, begin to live the new life." (January 25, 1987)

"Today, I want to wrap all of you in my mantle and lead you all on the road to *conversion*. Dear children, I beg you to hand over all your past life to the Lord and to surrender all the evil that has accumulated in your hearts to the Lord. I want each one of you to be happy but, with sin, no happiness is possible. Pray and you will know in prayer the new way of joy. Joy will reveal itself to your heart; and so, you will be the joyful witnesses

137

of what my Son and I expect from each one of you." (February 25, 1987)

"Dear children, I do not want you to remain in sins that displease me while you live the messages. Therefore, I want each one of you to live the new life and not to destroy all that God is creating in you and gives to you." (March 25, 1987)

"Dear children, I invite everyone to start living in God's love. Dear children, you are ready to commit sin and to put yourselves in the hands of Satan without any forethought. I call on you so that each one of you may knowingly decide in favor of God against Satan. I am your Mother and, therefore, I want to lead you all towards total holiness." (May 25, 1987)

"Dear children, I wish to lead you on the path of *conversion* and I want you to *convert* the world, and that your life may be *conversion* for others. Our Lady said, that from today, She is granting us special graces, She is giving us especially a gift of *conversion* so that each one of us may take the blessing to our homes and truly encourage others to *conversion*." (Reported by Marija on June 24, 1987)

"I bless you with the blessing of God and I beg you, dear children, to follow and to live my way. I love you, dear children. This is the reason why I have called you I don't know how many times, and I thank you for all you do for my intentions." (June 25, 1987)

"Dear children, today I invite you so that each one of you may decide to live the messages." (August 25, 1987)

"Dear children, today I want to call all of you so that each one of you may choose Paradise. The way is difficult for those who have not chosen God. Make up your mind, dear children, and believe that God offers himself to you in His fullness." (October 25, 1987)

"Dear children, today I invite each one of you to decide again to surrender everything to Me. It is only in this way that, in My turn, I may present each one of you to God." (November 27, 1987)

"I invite you to a total *conversion*; this is difficult for those who have not chosen God. I invite you, dear children, to a total *conversion* in God." (January 25, 1988)

"I am with you, I rejoice over your *conversion* and I shield you with my motherly cloak." (April 25, 1988)

Fasting

"I would like the people to pray with Me these days. As much as possible, they must *fast* rigorously on Wednesdays and Fridays, pray at least the Rosary each day while meditating on the joyful, the sorrowful and the glorious mysteries." (August 14, 1984)

"Today, I invite you to begin to *fast* with the heart. There are many people who *fast* but only because they see others *fasting*. *Fasting* has become a habit that no one wants to break. I am asking the parish to *fast* in thanksgiving to God for having allowed Me to remain this long in this parish. Dear children, pray and *fast* with your heart." (September 20, 1984)

"I thank you for all your prayers and sacrifices. I want to tell you, dear children, to live again the messages I give you. Especially revive *fasting* because with *fasting* you will rejoice Me and obtain that the Lord's project for Medjugorje may be entirely realized." (September 26, 1985)

"Today again, I invite you to prayer and *fasting*. Know, dear children, that with your help I can do everything and prevent Satan from misleading you and force him to go away from this place." (September 4, 1986)

"For this reason, dear children, pray constantly and purify your hearts in penance and *fasting*." (December 4, 1986)

Love

"I have already told you that I have chosen you in a special way such as you are. I, the Mother, I *love* you all. And at any moment, when things are difficult, do not fear. For I *love* you even when you are far away from Me and my Son. I ask you not to let my heart shed tears of blood because of the souls which are losing themselves through sin. Therefore, dear children, pray, pray, pray.'' (May 24, 1984)

"I thank you for offering all your afflictions to God and especially at this moment when He is trying you through the fruits that you are reaping. Know, dear children, that He *loves* you and, because of that, He tests you. Always offer all your burdens to God and do not worry." (October 11, 1984)

"You are a chosen people and the Lord has given you many graces. You are not aware of every message I am giving you. Now, I only wish to tell you this: pray, pray, pray. I don't know what else to tell you because I *love* you and I wish that in prayer you may come to know my *Love* and the *Love* of God." (November 15, 1984)

"No, you don't know yet how to *love* and you do not listen with *love* to the words I give you. Be aware, my beloved, that I am your Mother and that I have come on earth to teach you how to listen with *love*, how to pray with *love* and not because you are compelled by the cross. Through the cross, God is glorified in every man." (November 29, 1984)

"You know that the season of Joy is drawing near and that without *love*, you can obtain nothing. Therefore, first begin to *love* your family, the people of the parish, and then you will be able to *love* and accept all those who will come here. Let this week be the week during which you will learn to *love*." (December 13, 1984)

"Today also, I would like to thank you for all your sacrifices, and I address very special thanks to those who have become dear to my heart and who willingly come here. There are some parishioners who do not listen to the messages, but because of those who, in a special way, are close to my heart, because of them, I give messages to the parish. And I will continue to give some because I *love* you and I wish you to spread my messages with your heart." (January 10, 1985)

140

"Day after day, I have called you to a renewal and to prayer in your parish, but you do not accept that. Today, I am inviting you for the last time. This is Lent and you, during this season, can be moved for the sake of my *love* to respond to my call. If you do not do that, I do not wish to give you any more messages. God is allowing Me to do that." (February 21, 1985)

"Today, I am inviting you to live these words during this week: "I *love* God." Dear children, you will obtain everything through *Love,* even what you believe to be impossible. God wants this parish to belong to Him completely. I also wish this to be so." (February 28, 1985)

"During these coming days, people of all nationalities will come to the parish. And now, I invite you to *love. Love* first of all the members of your own family, and then you will be able to accept and *love* all those who come." (June 6, 1985)

"Today, I am giving you a message to call you to humility. During these recent days, you have felt a great joy because of all the people who were coming and you have told them your experiences with *love.* Now, I invite you to continue speaking with humility, with a heart open to all those who are passing here." (June 28, 1985)

"I thank you for every sacrifice you have made. And now, I urge you to offer all your acts of self-denial with *love.* I want those who are at a loss to confidently help the pilgrims, and the Lord will give them inasmuch as they have trusted." (July 4, 1985)

"Today, I bless you and I want to tell you that I *love* you. I appeal to you to live my messages. Today, I bless you all with the solemn blessing that the Almighty has granted Me." (August 15, 1985)

"Today, I would like to tell you that the Lord wants to put you through a test, but you can overcome it with prayer. God puts you through a test in your everyday work. Now, pray that you might overcome every trial. In all the trials God allows, come out of them more open to Him and come closer to Him with greater *love.*" (August 22, 1985)

"There is a time for every thing. Today, I invite you to begin to work on your hearts. All the work in the fields is completed. You find time to clean up the most forsaken places, but you leave your hearts aside. Be more industrious and, with *love,* clean up every corner of your hearts." (October 17, 1985)

"Day by day, I want to clothe you in holiness, goodness, obedience and *love* of God, so that, from day to day, you may be more beautiful and more prepared for your Lord. Dear children, listen to my messages and put them into practice. I want to guide you." (October 24, 1985)

"Today, I invite you to work in the Church. I *love* you all with a same *love* and I want everyone to do his best. I know, dear children, that you can do so, but you do not want to because you feel small and weak. Have courage and with little flowers, contribute to the holiness of the Church and to the good pleasure of Jesus." (October 31, 1985)

"I invite you to the *love* of your neighbors, especially those who hurt you. Then, you will be able to judge the intentions of hearts with *love.* Pray and *love,* dear children. With the power of *love,* you will be able to accomplish things which appear impossible to you." (November 7, 1985)

"This time is especially for you of this parish. During the summer, you say you have much work to do. Now that there is no work to do in the fields, work on yourselves. Come to Mass, as this time is given for you. Dear children, there are so many who come regularly in spite of bad weather, for they *love* Me and they want to show Me their *love* in a special way. I ask you to show Me your *love* by coming to Mass. The Lord will reward you generously." (November 21, 1985)

"I invite you to prepare yourselves for the feast of Christmas by penance, prayer and acts of *love.* Dear children, do not be absorbed with material things, because you would then be unable to experience the feast of Christmas." (December 5, 1985)

"Today, I would like to invite you to *love* your neighbor. If you were willing to *love* your neighbor, you would more deeply experience Jesus, especially on Christmas Day. God will grant you great gifts if you surrender yourselves to Him. On Christmas Day, I would like to give my special blessing, a maternal one, to the mothers and Jesus will give His blessing to all the others.'' (December 19, 1985)

"I want to thank all of you who have listened to my messages and who have lived what I requested on Christmas Day. From this day onward, you are purified from sin and I would like to continue guiding you in *love*. Abandon your hearts to Me.'' (December 26, 1985)

"Today also, I invite you to prayer; I need your prayers so that God may be glorified through all of you. Dear children, I beg of you to listen and accept my motherly invitation. I invite you, moved by *love*, so that I can help you.'' (January 16, 1986)

"I am asking you to live the Lent by making little sacrifices. Thank you for every sacrifice you have offered to Me. Dear children, continue to live this way. With *love*, help Me to present the offering; God will reward you for this.'' (March 13, 1986)

"I wish to thank you for all your sacrifices and I invite you to a greater sacrifice, the sacrifice of *love*. Without *love*, you cannot be a witness of your experience to others. For that reason, I invite you, dear children, to begin to live the *love* in your hearts.'' (March 27, 1986)

"I wish to invite you to live the Holy Mass. There are many among you who have felt the beauty of the Mass, but there are others who come unwillingly. I have chosen you, dear children, but Jesus gives His graces during Mass. Because of that, live the Holy Mass consciously. May each attendance to Mass be full of joy for you. Come with *love* and accept the Holy Mass.'' (April 3, 1986)

"I wish to invite you to grow in *love*. A flower cannot normally grow without water; similarly with you, dear children, you cannot grow without the divine blessing. You must necessarily seek day by day the blessing of God in order to grow normally and to accomplish all your work with God.'' (April 10, 1986)

143

"You are responsible for these messages. The source of grace is here. You are, dear children, the vessels which transmit the gifts. Therefore, dear children, I invite you to work at your task with a sense of responsibility. Everyone will be accountable according to his own measure. Give with *love* withholding nothing for yourselves." (May 8, 1986)

"Today, I am giving you my *love*. You don't know, dear children, how great my *love* is and you don't know how to accept it. In various ways, I want to show it to you but you don't recognize it. You don't understand my words with your heart and so you cannot understand my *love*. Dear children, accept Me in your life and you will be able to accept all I tell you and all that to which I invite you." (May 22, 1986)

"I invite you to live the *love* for God and for your neighbor. Without *love,* dear children, you can do nothing. Here is why I invite you to live in mutual *love*. Only then will you be able to *love* and accept Me and all those around you, all those who come to your parish. All will perceive my *love* through you. This is the reason why I beg you, dear children, beginning today, start to *love* with a burning *love,* the *love* with which I *love* you." (May 29, 1986)

"Today, I am calling you to holiness. You cannot live without holiness. This is the reason why with *LOVE* you triumph over every sin; with *LOVE,* you overcome also all the difficulties which present themselves. Dear children, I beg you to live *love*." (July 10, 1986)

"On this day, I invite you to meditate on the reasons why I have been so long with you. I am the mediator between you and God. Therefore, I invite you to live always out of *love* all that God expects from you. Dear children, in all humility, live all the messages I give you." (July 17, 1986)

"Hatred breeds dissension and it sees neither people nor things. I invite you to always spread understanding and peace, dear children, wherever you live. Act with *love*. May your only means of defence always be *love*. Through *love,* change to good all that Satan wants to destroy and appropriate for himself. Only then, will you belong totally to Me and I will be able to help you." (July 31, 1986)

"I thank you for the *love* you are showing Me. You know, dear children, that I *love* you without limit and that, from day to day, I pray the Lord to help you understand the *love* I show you. For this, dear children, pray, pray, pray." (August 21, 1986)

"Dear children, dedicate yourselves to prayer with a special *love*; and so, God will be able to give you graces." (October 2, 1986)

"Again today, I want to show you how much I *love* you, but I am sorry I cannot help each one of you to understand my *love*." (October 16, 1986)

"Live all the messages I give you out of *love* for Me." (October 30, 1986)

"Every soul needs prayers and graces to reach God and to develop the *love* of God." (November 6, 1986)

"Again today, I invite you to live and to follow with a particular *love* all the messages I give you... You know that I *love* you and that I burn with *love* for you. Therefore, dear children, commit yourselves to *love* so that day by day you may burn with *love* for God and that you may know better the *love* of God for you. Dear children, decide in favor of the *love* of God so that *love* may always come first in all of you." (November 20, 1986)

"Again today, I invite you to dedicate your life to Me with *love* so that I may guide you with *love*. I *love* you, dear children, with a special *love* and I want to lead you all to heaven." (November 27, 1986)

"Therefore, dear children, pray without stopping and put all the messages I give you into practice, for I am doing this with great *love* for God and for you." (January 1, 1987)

"I invite each one of you to begin to live, starting from today, the life that God expects from you. Continue to do works of *love* and of mercy." (March 25, 1987)

"Dear children, I invite everyone of you to start living in God's *love*." (May 25, 1987)

"Today I want to call all of you so that each one of you may choose Paradise. The way is difficult for those who have not chosen God. Make up your minds, dear children, and believe that God offers himself to you in His fulness. You are chosen and you must respond to the call of the Father who is inviting you through Me. Pray, for in prayer, each one of you will be able to reach perfect *love*." (October 25, 1987)

"You know that I *love* you without limit and that I want each one of you for Myself; but God has given a free will to everyone. I respect it with *love* and I humbly bow before it... I wish everything God has made for this parish to come true, but if you don't pray, you cannot discover my *love* and the plan God has for this parish and for each one of you... I am with you and I wish you to believe that I *love* you." (November 25, 1987)

"You know that I *love* you and that it is through *love* that I come here to show you the way of peace and of the salvation for your soul." (February 25, 1988)

"Dear children, you are not aware with what *love* God *loves* you." (March 25, 1988)

"I want you to *love* everyone, the good and the bad, with My *love*. Only in this way will *Love* rule the world. Dear children, I *love* you and I want you to surrender yourselves to Me so that I may lead you to God." (May 25, 1988)

The Family

"This evening, I would like to tell you to pray during this novena so that the Holy Spirit may come down on your *families* and your parish. Pray, you will not be sorry that you did. God will grant you gifts for which you will magnify Him until the end of your life." (June 2, 1984)

"With your prayers, you have helped Me carry out my plans.

Pray yet more that they may be totally fulfilled. I ask the *families* of the parish to recite the Rosary together in their *family*." (September 27, 1984)

"Today, I am asking you to read the Holy Bible in your homes every day and to place it in evidence so that you will remember to read it and to pray." (October 18, 1984)

"Today, I invite you to a renewal of prayer in your homes. The work in the fields is over. Now devote yourselves to prayer. May prayer hold the first place in your *families*." (November 1, 1984)

"During these coming days, I invite you to *family* prayer. In the name of God, I have given you messages many times, but you have not listened to me. This Christmas will be unforgettable for you provided you accept the messages that I give you. Dear children, do not let this day of Joy be the saddest day for Me." (December 6, 1984)

"The season of Joy is drawing near and without love, you can obtain nothing. Therefore, first of all, begin to love your *family* and the people of the parish and then you will be able to love and accept all those who will come here. Let this week be the week during which you will learn to love." (December 13, 1984)

"Today, I invite you to do something practical for Jesus Christ. I would like every *family* of the parish to bring Me a flower as a sign of surrender until the day of Joy. I would like each member of the *family* to place his flower beside the crib so that Jesus may come and see your total surrender to Him." (December 20, 1984)

"Today is the day I give the messages for the parish, but not all in the parish accept the messages and put them into practice. I am sad and, dear children, I would like you to listen to Me and to live my messages. Every *family* must make the *family* prayer and read the Bible." (February 14, 1985)

"I invite you to renew prayer in your *families*. Dear children, encourage the very young to pray and to go to Holy Mass." (March 7, 1985)

"Today, I wish to remind you: pray, pray, pray! In prayer you will come to know the greatest joy and the means of resolving all situations which seem to be without solutions. Thank you for progressing in prayer. Every individual is dear to my heart and I thank all those among you who have rekindled prayer in your *family*." (March 28, 1985)

"I invite you to place more blessed objects in your homes and that each one wear some blessed object on himself. Let all the objects be blessed. For then, Satan will not tempt you so much because you will be armed against him." (July 18, 1985)

"I want to tell you that, during these days, the Cross must be the center of your life. Pray especially before the Cross, from which flow great graces. Now, in your homes, make a special consecration to the Cross. Promise that you will offend neither Jesus nor the Cross nor blaspheme Him." (September 12, 1985)

"Today, I am inviting you to pray. Dear children, you forget that you are all important. The elderly especially are important in the *family*. Incite them to pray. May all the young people be a living example for others and may they be a witness of Jesus. Dear children, I beg you to begin to change through prayer and you will know what you must do." (April 24, 1986)

"I beg you to begin to change your life within the *family*. May the *family* be a flower of harmony that I may offer to Jesus. Dear children, may every *family* be active in prayer so that someday we may also see its fruits in the *family*. Then I will offer you all as petals to Jesus for the realization of the plans of God." (May 1, 1986)

"I rejoice because of those among you who are on the way to holiness. I invite you, by your testimony, to help all those who don't know how to live in a saintly manner. Therefore, dear children, may your *family* be the place where holiness is born. Help everyone to live in a saintly manner but, especially, all the members of your own *family*." (July 24, 1986)

Satan

"During the coming days, *Satan* wants to thwart all my plans. Pray so that his scheme does not come about. I shall pray my Son Jesus that He may give you the grace to see His victory over *Satan's* temptations." (July 12, 1984)

"During these coming days, you have felt how *Satan* works. I am always with you. Do not be afraid of temptations for God is always watching over you. I have given Myself up to you and I sympathize with you even in the least of your trials." (July 19, 1984)

"Pray because *Satan* is constantly trying to thwart my plans. Pray with the heart and offer yourselves to Jesus in prayer." (August 11, 1984)

"This Christmas, *Satan* wanted to interfere with God's plans in a special way. Dear children, you have recognized *Satan* even on Christmas Day. But God triumphed in all your hearts. May your hearts continue to be joyful." (December 27, 1984)

Message given to Vicka: "My dear children, *Satan* is so powerful and he uses all his power to obstruct my plans for you. Pray, pray constantly, and do not stop doing so for one moment. I too will pray my Son so that all my plans may be fulfilled. Be patient and perseverant in your prayers! Do not let yourselves be discouraged by *Satan*. He is very powerful in this world. Be cautious." (January 14, 1985)

"These days, *Satan* is deviously fighting against this parish and you, dear children, have fallen asleep in prayer and few are those who go to Mass. Persevere in these days of trials." (January 17, 1985)

"These days, you were able to savor the sweetness of God through the renewal which has taken place in this parish. *Satan* wants to work yet harder to take away joy that is in each one of you. Through prayer, you can disarm him completely and assure your happiness." (January 24, 1985)

"I am calling you to a more active prayer and to a greater participation in the Mass. I want the Mass to be an experience of God for you. I especially want to say to the young people: be open to the Holy Spirit because God wants to draw you to Himself in these times when *Satan* is active." (May 16, 1985)

"I urge you to invite everybody to the prayer of the Rosary. With the Rosary, you will overcome all the difficulties that *Satan* wants to inflict on the Catholic Church. You, priests, pray the Rosary, devote some time to the Rosary." (June 25, 1985)

"I love this parish and I protect it with my mantle from all the wiles of *Satan*. Pray that *Satan* may flee away from the parish and from every individual who comes to the parish. This way, you will be able to hear every call from God and respond to it with your life." (July 11, 1985)

"I invite you to place more blessed objects in your homes and that each one wear some blessed objects on himself. Let all the objects be blessed. For then, *Satan* will not tempt you so much because you will be armed against Him." (July 18, 1985)

"I want to tell you that I have chosen this parish and that I keep it in my hands like a little flower that does not want to die. I invite you to surrender yourselves to Me so that I may offer you, pure and without sin, to God. *Satan* has taken over a part of the plan and wants to make it his own. Pray that he might not succeed because I want you for Myself so I can offer you to God." (August 1, 1985)

"Today, I invite you, and especially now, to begin already the combat against *Satan* with prayer. Now that he is aware of my activity, *Satan* wishes to work harder. Arm yourselves against *Satan* and, with the Rosary in your hand, you will triumph." (August 8, 1985)

"I invite you to prayer, especially now when *Satan* wants to use the harvests of your vineyards. Pray that he might not succeed in carrying out his plan." (August 29, 1985)

"Today, I thank you for all your prayers. Pray continuously

and even more so that *Satan* may go away far from this place. Dear children, *Satan's* project has fallen through. Pray that God's plan may be realized in this parish. I especially thank the young people for the sacrifices they have offered.'' (September 5, 1985)

"I invite you to help Jesus with your prayers for the realization of all the plans He has already begun to carry out here. Offer your sacrifices to Jesus so that He may fulfill all He has planned and so that *Satan* may not be able to do anything.'' (January 9, 1986)

"Today, I invite you to pray for the realization of God's plans and His wishes for you. Help others to convert themselves, especially all those who come to Medjugorje. Dear children, do not let *Satan* become the master of your hearts because, in this case, you will become the image of *Satan* and not of Me. I invite you to pray so that you may be witnesses of my presence. Without you, the Lord cannot realize all He wishes. The Lord has given you all a free will and you may dispose of it as you wish.'' (January 30, 1986)

"Hatred breeds dissension and it sees neither people nor things. I invite you to always spread understanding and peace, dear children, wherever you live. Act with love. May your only means of defense always be love. Through love, change to good all that *Satan* wants to destroy and appropriate for himself. Only then, you will belong totally to Me and I will be able to help you.'' (July 31, 1986)

"You know what I have promised you: an oasis, an oasis of peace but you ignore that around every oasis there is a desert where *Satan* keeps watch and wants to try each one of you. Dear children, it is only through prayer that you may overcome the influence of *Satan*. Wherever you are, I am present, but I cannot take your liberty away from you.'' (August 7, 1986)

"Today, again, I invite you to prayer and fasting. Know, dear children, that with your help I can do everything and prevent *Satan* from misleading you and even force him to go away from this place. Dear children, *Satan* lies in wait for each one of you. He especially wants to sow the seeds of suspicion in each one of you in everyday things. Therefore, I invite you to make of your day nothing but prayer and total surrender to God." (September 4, 1986)

"Therefore, I call you through prayer and your life to help destroy all that is evil in men and to discern the lie that *Satan* uses to lose souls." (September 25, 1986)

"This is why, dear children, I invite you to prayer and to total surrender to God because *Satan* wishes to win you over in everyday affairs and take first place in your life." (October 16, 1986)

"Dear children, you are ready to commit sin and to put yourselves in the hands of *Satan* without any forethought. I call on you so that each one of you may knowingly decide in favor of God against *Satan*. I am your Mother and because of that I wish to lead you all to total holiness." (May 25, 1987)

"Dear children, I beg you to take up the ways of holiness today. I love you and I want you to be holy. I do not want *Satan* to block you on that way." (July 25, 1987)

"Dear children, *Satan* is strong and he lies in wait to tempt each one of you. Pray so that he will be able neither to harm you nor to block you on the way to holiness." (September 25, 1987)

"Pray that *Satan* may not entice you with his pride and deceitful power. (November 25, 1987)

"I wish you to obey Me and not let *Satan* seduce you. Dear children, *Satan* is very strong. For this reason, I ask you to offer Me your prayers for the salvation of those under his influence. Be a witness by your way of life and offer it as a sacrifice for the salvation of the world. I am with you and I thank you for this. When in heaven, you will receive from the Father the reward he has promised you. For this reason, little children, do not be afraid. If you pray, *Satan* cannot harm you, for you are children of God and He is the One watching over you. Pray; and may you always keep the Rosary in your hands as a sign that you belong to Me, a sign against *Satan*.." (February 25, 1988)

"Pray together so that the *Devil* may not sway you as the wind does the reed... Pray constantly so that the *Devil* may not take advantage of you. Pray that you may be able to understand that you belong to Me. I bless you with the Blessing of Joy." (May 25, 1988)

Holiness

"Dear children, if you live the messages, you will foster the growth of the seeds of *holiness*. As a Mother, I call all of you to *holiness* so that you may radiate it to others. You are like a mirror for the people." (October 10, 1985)

"I invite you to decide entirely in favor of God. I beg you, dear children, to give yourselves totally and you will be able to live all I tell you. It will not be difficult for you to surrender yourselves completely to God." (January 2, 1986)

"Today, I am calling you to *holiness*. You cannot live without *holiness*. This is the reason why, with LOVE, triumph over every sin; with LOVE, overcome also all the difficulties which present themselves." (July 10, 1986)

"I rejoice because of those among you who are on the way to *holiness*. I invite you, by your testimony, to help all those who don't know how to live in a saintly manner. Therefore, dear children, may your family be a place where *holiness* is born. Help everyone to live a *saintly* manner, but especially, all the members of your own family." (July 24, 1986)

"You know that I want to guide you on the way to *holiness*. But I do not want to oblige you to become *holy* by force. I wish that everyone of you, by his little sacrifices, help himself and help Me so I may guide you and you may increase in *holiness* from day to day. Consequently, dear children, I do not force you to live my messages, but this prolonged time visiting with you is a sign that I love you immeasurably and I wish each one of you to be *holy*." (October 9, 1986)

"Today also, I invite you all to pray with all your heart and to change your life from day to day. I especially invite you, dear children, to begin a life of *holiness* with your prayers and your sacrifices, for I want each one of you, who has drawn from this source of grace, to reach Paradise. Therefore, dear children, pray and from day to day, change your life in order to be *holy.*" (November 13, 1986)

"Dear children, it is to teach you to walk in the way of *holiness* that I have remained so long with you. Therefore, dear children, pray without stopping and put all the messages I give you into practice for I am doing this with great love for God and for you." (January 1, 1987)

"Dear children,... I am your Mother and, therefore, I want to lead all of you towards total *holiness.*" (May 25, 1987)

"I beg you to take up the way of *holiness* today. I love you and I want you to be *holy.* I do not want Satan to stop you on that way. Dear children, pray and accept everything God is offering you on this bitter way, for to the one who begins to walk in this path, God reveals all his sweetness and this one will respond more willingly to each call from God. Do not attach importance to little things and reach heaven." (July 25, 1987)

"Dear children, again today, I invite you all so that each one of you may decide to live the messages. God has also allowed Me this year which the Church has dedicated to Me to speak to you and to urge you on to *holiness.* Dear children, ask God the graces which He gives you through Me. I am ready to obtain from God all you ask so that your *holiness* may be complete." (August 25, 1987)

"Satan is strong and he lies in wait to tempt each one of you. Pray so that he will be able neither to harm you nor block you on the way of *holiness.*" (September 25, 1987)

"God wants to make *saints* of you. For this reason, He is calling you to a total surrender through Me... May your way of life be rather a testimony on the way of *holiness.*" (April 25, 1988)

Peace

"Today I thank you and I wish to invite you all to the *peace* of God. I wish each one of you may experience in his heart this *peace* that God gives." (June 25, 1987)

"You know that I love you and that it is through love that I come here to show you the way of *peace* and of the salvation of your souls." (February 25, 1988)

"He (God) allows Me to be with you to teach you and to help you find the way of *Peace*." (March 25, 1988)

The church[1]

"Take time to come closer to God in the *church*. Come to the *house of your Father*. Remember your deceased. Give them joy through the Mass." (January 28, 1987)

"May the Holy Mass be LIFE for you. Be aware that the *church* is God's palace, a place where I gather you and want to show you the way leading to God. Come and pray; don't watch how the others are and behave and don't speak ill of them. May your life be rather a testimony on the way of holiness. The *churches* are worthy of respect and are consecrated, for God who became Man dwells there day and night. Therefore, my little children, believe and pray that the Father may increase your faith; then you may ask what you need. I am with you, I rejoice over your conversion and I shield you with my motherly cloak." (April 25, 1988)

Total surrender

"My Son, Jesus Christ, wants to bestow special graces on you through Me. My Son is rejoiced by your *surrender*." (May 17, 1984)

---

1. The building, the place.

"Today, I invite you to do something practical for Jesus Christ. I would like every family of the parish to bring me a flower as a sign of *surrender* until the day of Joy. I would like each member of the family to place his flower beside the crib so that Jesus may come and see your total *surrender* to Him." (December 20, 1984)

"May your prayer become the sign of your *surrender* to God." (June 13, 1985)

"I invite you to *surrender* yourselves to Me so that I may offer you, pure and without sin, to God." (August 1, 1985)

"God will grant you great gifts if you *surrender* yourselves to Him." (December 19, 1985)

"I invite you to decide entirely in favor of God. I beg you, dear childlren, to *give* yourselves *totally* and you will be able to live all I tell you. It will not be difficult for you to *surrender* yourselves completely to God." (January 2, 1986)

"I invite you to make of your day nothing but prayer and *total surrender* to God." (September 4, 1986)

"Today also, I invite each one of you to decide again to *surrender* everything to Me. It is only in this way that, in My turn, I may present each one of you to God." (November 25, 1987)

"God can give you all you ask of Him. But you seek God only when illness, problems and difficulties come to you, and you think that God keeps far away from you, that He neither listens to you nor answers your prayers. No, dear children, this is not true. If you are far away from God, you cannot receive graces for you do not ask for them with a firm FAITH. I pray for you from day to day. I want to draw you closer and closer to God but I cannot do this if you do not want. In order to do that, dear children, *put your lives* in the hands of God." (January 25, 1988)

"I want to call you to prayer and to a *total surrender* to God. You know that I love you and that it is through love that I come here in order to show you the way of peace and that of the salvation of your soul." (February 25, 1988)

"Today also I am inviting you to a *total surrender* to God. Dear children, you are not aware with what love God loves you. This is the reason why He allows Me to be with you in order to teach you and to help you find the way of Peace. But you cannot find this way if you do not pray. Consequently, dear children, leave everything and *dedicate* all your time to God. Then He will grant you gifts and bless you. Little children, do not forget that your life is fleeting like the spring flower so beautiful today and totally disappeared tomorrow. Therefore, PRAY so that your prayer and your *surrender* to God may become a sign. Thus your testimony will be of value not only to yourselves but to everyone throughout eternity." (March 25, 1988)

"God... is calling you to a *total surrender* through Me." (April 25, 1988)

"I invite you to a *total surrender* to God... Dear children, you are Mine, I love you and I want you to *surrender* yourselves to Me in order that I may lead you to God." (May 25, 1988)

Part Five

Testimony of Flaminio Piccoli

Speaking of Medjugorje and in relation to its events, we could quote thousands of similar experiences which bear witness to and describe the states of one's soul which are experienced there in prayer and in the encounter with God.

We have chosen to give the testimony of an eminent man who went to Medjugorje as a simple pilgrim. A middle-aged man, he is an *Italian ex-minister and, now, president of the International Union of the Christian Democratic Parties of the whole world: Flaminio Piccoli*. He went twice to Medjugorje as an anonymous pilgrim. He described his experience in a public declaration which he himself entitled: "My Testimony".

Here is what he says: "Some Catholic newspapers have aroused uneasiness and disarray among the people who, through immediate knowledge, have been convinced that an extraordinary phenomenon is going on in Medjugorje. That is why I think it would be of some use to describe the experience I lived there on two occasions as well as my encounters with the Franciscans and the visionaries of Medjugorje.

"Medjugorje appeared to me as a place of exceptional serenity where nothing jars the atmosphere! A total authenticity in faith and worship, a spontaneity and an absence of constraint truly touched me. I saw there, among the people, a profound desire for prayer and meditation which penetrates their conscience and leads them to conversion.

"I had the privilege of attending the apparitions. They are not suggestive, but I declare that we feel we are in face of a 'qualitative leap' when we are in the presence of these visionaries. Their behavior is one of deep recollection, free from any influence from the setting around them.

"We notice the same behavior in the people who surround them. The expression of these visionaries suddenly changes when they are rapt in ecstasy. During the apparition, each one of them is recollected in his own way. Their attitude during the ecstasy is personal and proper to each one of them. A young girl was showing signs of joy and happiness beyond description while the other looked sad. The youngest of the boys (Jakov) looked very serious, a contrast with the sympathetic and lively behavior he displays in everyday life, like any other boy of his age.

"Before me, an extraordinary event was unfolding itself! During my first visit, as I was coming out of the church, a young man approached me and said: 'Honorable Piccoli, I am a communist. I happen to be here today and I prayed for you...' I was stunned! I answered him: 'As for me, I prayed for my country.' This young man is a sociologist. A profound human relationship was established between us. His letters fill me with joy and I find there a sound experience of faith."

The Sons of Saint Francis

"I had the opportunity of meeting the Franciscan fathers who are in charge of the parish. One of them, Father Tomislav, had blessed my home during his stay in a suburb of Rome, in a parish where he was helping in pastoral work. I did not hear them make a single critical remark about the bishop. All of them reflect a profound spirituality, express a great peace and display much sensitivity in pastoral work. In spite of everything, the bishop declared: 'We are placed before a case of collective hallucinations'. Meanwhile, no accusation against two Franciscans was ever proved. None, nor has the least declaration shown that it was a matter of 'manipulations' or of 'magic' exercised on the millions of faithful who go there. The truth is altogether different from this! Various medical investigations led by scientific experts, who are not always arrogant, have proved that, at Medjugorje, an extraordinary mystery is taking place before which science is helpless. This mystery bears real and concrete fruits: conversion, life of prayer, authentic penance, profound teaching received by the pilgrims either from the testimony of the parishioners or by Mary's messages. These messages hold such a power in their simplicity that they disarm us and make us see our spiritual poverty. They give remedies to the greatest ills and to the most dangerous deviations from which mankind suffers."

And the Future?

"I shall go back to Medjugorje. As man and Christian, I try to penetrate the profound meaning of the messages of Mary who asks each one of us to go to the limit of our own duty. We too are responsible for the evil in the world. Any immoral act is in reality an act of war. It does not arise from an American or a Soviet, but from a series of mistakes, of moral violations, of little and great immoral acts for which each man, each woman, each young and not so young person is responsible. All together and each for himself.

"In Medjugorje, an urgent motherly call has been made to remind us of our own responsibility. There, a great spiritual richness is manifested; it offers the pilgrims an extraordinary strength to confront the life of today. This is the testimony I wanted to present to all the readers. I am not a "perverter of the truth". I consider that all of us who have gone to this small Croatian village provide an additional proof of the authenticity of the apparitions. This faith, sustained throughout the centuries, has given us strength in suffering, perseverance in work, and an unshakable hope. The scientific atheists, who were filled with doubts when they went to Medjugorje, recognized in these wonderful events something extraordinary which escapes science. Therefore, is it too much to ask the Christian Italian media to open their ears to this 'people of God' while waiting for the Church to pronounce her judgment on this extraordinary event, this phenomenon which converts atheists, strengthens believers and offers everyone a profound sense of the Christian mysteries which are at the root of all our commitments?''

In the Name of Hundreds of Others, Milona Speaks

We could say that this is just a witness among so many others but, yet, she is a chosen witness.

This witness is Milona Habsburg, born in 1958 in Munich in the Federal Republic of Germany. She is a descendant in direct line from the Habsburg kings. She is a beautiful girl who has attended several faculties and obtained, among others, a diploma from the University of Paris in 1982. She speaks six languages fluently (German, French, English, Italian, Portuguese and Spanish). She is now learning Croatian.

Milona says she grew up with her six brothers and sisters in an ordinary Christian milieu. She was fortunate during her studies (particularly in Paris) in meeting an older priest who guided her closely in her spiritual life and helped her face the coming years with greater trust. At this time, she foresaw her future in terms of a good marriage and a profound family life. But while she was studying tourism, journalism and political sciences, she did not have much time to think about these things.

Milona's favorable circumstances during her studies (and even before) allowed her to travel all over Europe and visit her many royal relatives. She was thus able to broaden her knowledge of the world and of life around her. It was at this time that she heard of Medjugorje, in May 1984.

On June 23 of the same year, she found herself in Medjugorje. No particular inspiration nor special intention had drawn her there. She had joined a group of tourists making a bus trip organized by one of her cousins.

There was nothing extraordinary in this, she thought! But as soon as she arrived in Medjugorje, she soon began to change her mind. Three days later, she was no more the girl of yesterday. "Everything had changed in me", says Milona. She practically started all over again. Her concept of Christian life was not the same anymore. She, herself, was surprised at that!

"One could not say this was mere chance", thought Milona. She was becoming aware, especially after having attended one of the apparitions, that something *beyond description* had just taken place within herself. This something was growing stronger every day. She already felt that Jesus and Mary were not drawing her towards them, but even further within themselves! She was filled with an immense joy that was new to her, that she had never known!

Milona gives an account of all that was going on in her and how, all of a sudden, she discovered another reality. Once, when seated in the shadow of the large concrete cross on Mount Krizevac, she tells us she felt herself very much rooted to the "earth" but, inwardly, she "was becoming smaller and smaller with the sole wish of melting away in God".

After her first stay in Medjugorje, she returned home. A wonderful and extraordinary flame was burning in her heart, but she could not speak of this to anyone, neither to her brothers nor to her sisters who, it seems, would not have understood her. They could notice that something new and unusual was going on in her without being able, for all this, to know anymore about it. She was there, her heart filled with this new experience and yet unable to open up to them.

Things being as they were, she decided to go to Medjugorje again. And since then, with few intervals, she has been there practically all the time. If the number of days she spent in Medjugorje were counted, they would amount to more than five hundred. She admits she feels happier and happier. "I cannot describe what is going on in me", says Milona, "but I feel I am experiencing here an absolutely special encounter with Jesus and his Mother. Everything has changed in my life. One could say that my centers of interests have been reversed. Before that, Jesus and Mary were in my heart, but only as a part of my life as a whole. Now, everything revolves around them. This is unexpected! The will of Christ has become the motive of all my activities. I seek this will and I find it in His Mother Mary."

"Yes, how amazing", shouts Milona. "This change in me is miraculous. I see it also in the other *young people* who come here at Medjugorje. Most of them are there out of curiosity, sceptical, but they cannot resist the Power which is in action here. I have come here fifteen times and I happily spend here the greater part of my time, primarily to draw closer to Jesus and to His Mother Mary. I wish to accept all the graces which are offered to me. In the hope of not turning away from Her, I willingly prolong my stay."

When asked how she experienced being present at an apparition for the first time, Milona replies: "I recited the rosary with the others and I felt a deep peace. But, at the moment the Virgin Mary appeared, I was very moved and then I sincerely and completely surrendered myself to Her. I asked Her to free me from all anxiety and distress which weighed on my soul. I mumbled to Her unceasingly and with perseverance: 'Take everything, take everything.' Then, I felt that an infinite tenderness touched me and, at that moment, all the anxiety which had accumulated in me, disappeared. All this burden suddenly fell away! After that", mentions Milona, "for the first time, I was filled with joy and I could repeat: 'Source of our joys, pray for us' (an invocation from the Litanies)."

"For the first time, I really knew the meaning of joy. On that day, the Virgin Mary freed me from a great burden. I am sure She would do that for all those who ask for this in their heart. Since then, each day I live a new inner experience which, through the ups and downs of life, lead man always closer to his God."

"And so I think that here in Medjugorje, Mary, our Mother, will answer all the questions which young people can ask Her. She will make them understand where to find love, peace and serenity to which the human heart reaches out in the innermost part of itself. She will show them the direct way leading to Christ, the center of all life. To say the truth, this is not something altogether new, but, in some way, this revives us. We have already had similar experiences, but they were incomplete and cold. Here, we obtain answers we have looked for for a long time."

"For some time", Milona tells us, "the Virgin Mary has liberated me from strong inner pressures which were taking root in me. In plain words, I could not forgive the man I loved because he had done me some harm. In prayer and meditation, here at Medjugorje, I understood it was possible to forgive without any reservations whatsoever!"

"This happened during Mass. After the Eucharist, I asked Jesus to help me to forgive, that is, to do it in my place. Instantly, this difficulty disappeared. The inner tension in forgiving went away and I was able to forgive him with all my heart. For me, this was a giant step. I understood that it was necessary to acknowledge our own weaknesses to be able to forgive the weaknesses of others." "We just have to say", Milona tells us, " 'Lord, I cannot do it. Do it for me', and all will be settled."

"At Medjugorje", Milona continues, "I was enlightened as so many others were. I understand myself in my fall as in my ascent. Everything, from the greatest happiness to despair, from the feeling of being forsaken to that of security, all this I experienced at Medjugorje. This is not so simple, but everything is possible to the Lord."

Milona says that her life was completely changed at Medjugorje. Her aspirations, her plans in life are not the same anymore. Her deep wish to raise a family is being gradually replaced by the serious intention and the wish to enter a convent, a convent where the bonds with earthly things are severed and there remains only the desire to unite oneself to God in prayer, to the One who alone makes our happiness. This maturity grows from day to day. "Never", she says, "could we say that we have nothing to do today because we did much yesterday. If, each day, I fully live my encounter with the Lord, I shall keep on going in this path." To make progress, we must start over again every day. With Milona, we can repeat the old proverb: "Whoever does not progress, regresses." Besides, this is confirmed in everyday life.

Milona always likes to be present at the apparitions; even after two hundred apparitions, it is always new! For some time, she was responsible for keeping the room of the apparitions tidy.

"Now", she says, "I wait for the coming of the Virgin Mary with calm and serenity. For me, it means being together. Always different, but always beautiful." She says that the members of her family who come to Medjugorje from time to time feel something similar. Each time, they experience something deep and intimate. In a more special way, they experience and discover the messages of the Blessed Virgin. "The messages, these amazing words which come to us from on high, the more we live them, the more we are filled with joy."

Finally, Milona would like to tell all the young men and women of her age: "Do not burden yourselves with so much anxiety for the future, money, or work. One can live happily without worrying about that. At first sight, this may appear like living in the clouds, but if we abandon ourselves and if we persist in this way, life becomes a reality in which many things take second place."

"This is a question of life and all the rest is only a part of the road towards the goal which draws us and makes us happy. This is why I would like to make known, more particularly to the young people of my age, that you can be spared all hardship if you entrust yourselves sincerely to the Lord. He is the One, the Reality which fills the human heart and gives it peace. I know I am not expected to lecture you, but I would like to encourage young people to come to Medjugorje to discover the true way in the communion with Jesus and his Mother. Only, we must keep in mind that we don't go to Medjugorje as we go to a disco. Here we seek God who manifests himself and who gives himself willingly to those who truly want Him. This is the gift of Medjugorje. The happiness in Medjugorje consists in the grace we receive to sanctify ourselves, to open ourselves more easily to God, and to experience His Presence here as in no other place in the world. I would advise you to come here at least for three or four days to have this grace and this peace offered to you, a peace and a grace which visibly flow with such great power."

Janko Bubalo

"Mary, 'Health of the Sick'"

Few are the places where this invocation of the litanies of the sick can be said with as much sincerity as in Medjugorje. All we say and all we write on Medjugorje has value inasmuch as we discover how God and Mary work there and what they accomplish. It is becoming more and more obvious that there they renew men both physically and spiritually.

The unexpected healings occurring at the spiritual level are the most numerous and the most fruitful. There, the Virgin Mary in various ways prepares the hearts of men to receive God who always offers himself but does so more abundantly here. To know how the Virgin Mary does this, we could question hundreds and thousands of persons who were transformed there and who are not the same anymore.

Some of Father Rupćić's thoughts on this subject could help us to understand this. He says: "Medjugorje manifests itself more and more clearly as a place of conversion and of profound transformation of the people. This characteristic raises it above all other places of pilgrimage in the world. In all of Yugoslavia, and perhaps in the whole world, there does not exist a church which is daily attended by so many people who convert themselves, receive communion as the church of Medjugorje. Medjugorje, in spite of everything, confirms itself primarily by accepting the demands, sometimes exacting, of conversion, prayer, fasting and forgiveness. These are not always pleasant things to offer the pilgrims of Medjugorje, but they do not frighten people away. The demands are without compromise and are paid dearly, but they are accepted as a remedy. Millions of people from all over the world rush to find this remedy. The impressive number of pilgrims to this day runs up to between seven and eight millions. Sometimes, the number of pilgrims climbs to one hundred thousand a day! Among the pilgrims, there have been several thousand priests, some fifteen bishops and archbishops. In Medjugorje, one million and a half lay people have made a personal confession, the first in thirty, forty years and more for many.

"There is a very powerful element there that draws people from all the corners of the world. And this is not human motives, far from that, for the inaccessibility of the place, the poverty, the scarcity of water and of the most elementary hygienic conditions for a normal life; poor communications, a lack of accommodations, the opposition of the authorities, threats, discussions and the fact of being exposed to the disagreeable consequences of the above: all of this should have detrimental effects on the number of pilgrims. The true reason for this affluence of pilgrims lies uniquely in the intrinsic power of the call which God addresses from that place to all men. This call exercises such an attraction that it draws not only the Catholics but also all the Christians and even the non-Christians. Among them a certain number of unbaptized will return home after having received baptism. This irresistible call provokes a response from young people and elderly people, from the sick and the healthy. Many are those who will travel more than one hundred kilometers on foot to reach this place. Parents admit they are outdone by their children in the response to this call.

"At Medjugorje, the usual ceremonies associated with pilgrimages like candlelight processions and others do not exist. This does not prevent resounding prayer and many strong manifestations of Christian love from happening. The Church at Medjugorje displays the youthful strength and the enthusiasm of the early Church of Jerusalem. Religious ceremonies bring out no differences, still less contradictions, even though they are made up of various races, languages and cultures. Judging from appearances, we cannot distinguish a bishop or an archbishop from a priest, a religious from a lay person, a religious woman from a married one, a novice from a fiancée, a personality engaged in politics from a simple citizen, an owner of a firm or business from a laborer. All are of one heart and one soul (Ac 4:32) with an equal steadfastness in prayer and sharing of the bread (Ac 2:46). This is why the archbishop of Split, Msgr. Franić, will state in his declaration that nowhere else in the world, neither at Lourdes nor at Fatima, has he seen greater piety and that Medjugorje has done more for faith in Yugoslavia in three years than all the pastoral work of forty years.

"Those in Medjugorje who do not see the Virgin Mary directly, see her reflection on the visionaries and on the others who are present at the apparitions. The one who has not heard Her messages directly hears their echo in the hearts and sees the behavior of hundreds and of thousands of people. This has led someone to say: 'I do not know whether the Virgin Mary has appeared to the young visionaries but I see that She has appeared to those people there.' Someone else yet said: 'And if there were no proof to authenticate these apparitions of the Virgin Mary, these people would be one.'

"At Medjugorje, there are fewer and fewer people who come there out of curiosity. Physical healings are not given prime importance. Research aimed solely at miracles (physical healings) blind the eyes to the greater gifts of the Spirit one can receive. This is precisely the experience which transforms the man who is there out of curiosity into "the man who believes". The despaired obtain hope in goods far greater yet than those they first desired. At Medjugorje, people begin to see with the eyes of FAITH. And that changes everything. In faith, previous knowledge fades away and shows itself as inadequate, unilateral and incomplete. Faith makes our illnesses and our miseries more transparent. People realize here that it is better to recover faith than sight. Even if the disease is not cured, it loses its thorn and the sick receive the grace to accept their illness.

"Prayer, the reception of the sacraments, vigils and fasting prove that a change has come about, that the sick have been healed, that is, redeemed. We see the effects of repentance, conversion and purification on the pilgrims. Whatever does not change hearts here has no value. All those who thought otherwise have been dissuaded. No one looks for magic water or candles to obtain temporal favors or health anymore. If there are always some who keep on looking for these gifts, it is the sign that inner healing was received and this would be their way of thanking for the grace of conversion and a change of heart.

"People give up cheap, simple and easy means and seek those which will *radically* heal their heart, their intelligence and the paralysis of their blinded spirit. No, in Medjugorje, there is no magic in spite of the fact that there could easily be some. There, through the Virgin Mary, Christ does to the countless and incurable sick what He has already done once by saying: 'Your faith has saved you' (Lk 18:42). Magic has nothing to do with the change of life which ensues. Moreover, the inner healing testifies to the fact that it is not a matter of magic which would exploit God without producing any change in man. Here, people pray for conversion, discernment and the strength to carry their cross and follow Christ.

"No one leaves Medjugorje empty-handed or without any miracle in him. All go back home regenerated and bring a new heart, new arguments and new strength. The one who was not healed received the strength to transcend his difficulty. The 'I cannot' (of former days) forgive, bear suffering and illness, pray, change, give up drinking, stop blaspheming, reject old habits, be closer to husband or wife, was changed into a strong 'yes' in faith, this 'yes' which supersedes all that is negative and transforms it into good deeds and conversion. The one whose prayer was not answered has been rewarded with a profound joy; those who formerly wept and despaired about their destiny, have been convinced that they are not abandoned to some sort of fate and condemned to a meaningless death but, much to the contrary, are entitled to Life. This is why joy replaces tears and hope, despair. And those who have not obtained physical healing, give thanks; those who did not know how to pray, pray; those who were slaves to sin are liberated. These are the extraordinary experiences of all those who come through Medjugorje. This is why most pilgrims willingly come back to Medjugorje and remain there for days and months."

Medjugorje grows and develops itself more from the fact that human bodies are regenerated there. No one knows how many physical healings have occurred for Medjugorje does not attempt to justify itself by these healings. It lives from the grace that God and Mary abundantly lavish there. But we shall, nevertheless, tell you about a recent cure. It was told to us by the woman who was healed.

Her name, she said, is Agnes HEUPEL. She was born on January 29, 1951 at Munster in Westphalia in Western Germany. She completed her studies with a state diploma in nursing. She worked at Bad Kimuger, Kromach and Donsten, where she became ill suffering from osteoporosis while she was nursing a seriously ill patient. Her condition grew worse and it did not improve even after two serious operations. The paralysis of her limbs, which caused her pain, was becoming serious. Attempts were made to work on the source of the pain, but without success. With time, other complications developed, such as pains in the bladder and the intestines. Her only help was the use of two crutches which had been given to her. Surely, all kinds of solutions were tried but they were of no avail. She ended up by drawing the pension for invalids and there was nothing else to do, but to count her days.

How had she taken all that? Agnes lets us know in one sentence alone: "For me everything was finished." Two years before, Agnes had gone to Fatima. While there, when the priest had blessed her with the Blessed Sacrament, she had suddenly been able to kneel, but after that, everything had gone back to her previous condition, Agnes tells us. During these difficult days, her marriage, contracted on October 5, 1973, broke up at the time when she most needed help. Her husband had simply "forgotten" her from the very beginning of her illness. After her second operation, she returned home to live with her parents. Since she could not do anything, she began to read. She tells us she had even undertaken the study of theology. When asked if, at this time, she could "pray", Agnes replies: "Yes and no! During my unhappy marriage, I had simply lost the ability to relate to prayer. My husband did not want to pray and then..."

Agnes' health was taking a turn for the worse. Her diagnostic revealed a case of acute osteoporosis. Thus her days were slipping by without any hope of recovery. "On January 24, 1984, during my sleep, or perhaps drowsiness, I saw the Mother of God",

Agnes tells us. She was showing her a place with a white building and she was telling her: "Look at this, this is Medjugorje." This was the first time she was hearing about Medjugorje. Never could Agnes have thought of that on her own for she did not know Medjugorje. No one around her was speaking of that place. She was perplexed.

At the beginning of the month of March 1986, at Borghorst, Agnes attended a Mass celebrated by Father Slavko Barbarić. After Mass, she had spoken with this priest. Father Slavko had prayed over her. This was the first day since a long time that she had not wept. She was now thinking more and more of Medjugorje. On the first of May, after a long journey of four days, she reached her destination. She arrived during the evening office. She participated in the office with devotion especially during the prayer over the sick which is made everyday in Medjugorje. Then she went to look for accommodations.

Father Slavko was obviously her only support, but she quickly figured out her way about and soon had contacted some people. Day after day, she went to the church and prayed. She says she prayed much to prepare herself, as it were, for what was to happen to her, and at the same time, she would ask herself: "What do you want here? What are you looking for?" Such thoughts constantly kept stirring in her mind. Finally, the great day came, the 13th of May.

On the morning of the 13th of May, 1986, Father Slavko had given her the permission to be present at the evening apparition. Very moved by this invitation, Agnes wandered around the church practically all day. She prayed and meditated, but there was no one with whom she could share. Time was going by. It was already five in the afternoon, then half past five... The preparation for the apparition was beginning in prayer. "I felt totally exhausted", says Agnes. "I would have liked to turn back and run away. On the other hand, I wanted to be there. I wanted this at any cost. Finally, after much distress, I went up to the room of the apparitions. I was all perturbed, unable to pray. When the visionaries began to recite the rosary, I was not at all 'there'."

"And suddenly the moment of the apparition came. Feelings of uneasiness and nervousness vanished instantly. All of a sudden,

173

I was calm and I felt a cold sensation around my mouth. Then, I had sensations of burning, of prickling... At that moment, I was not praying for myself, I was praying for my relatives as I had promised I would. Then, from the divan where I was seated, I fell on my knees. I had not done that for a long time. I fell on my knees consciously, as if I were preparing the way for what was to follow... This is difficult to explain. Not that I saw anything! But in my innermost self, there were so many things going on... as it were, in slow motion. I had lost the notion of time.

— I was indifferent to everything around me.

— I felt somewhat isolated.

— Yes, totally isolated!"

— Then, what happened?

— "When that began to 'burn' on my face, I felt a hot current running through me from head to toe and over all my body... I don't know how to describe this phenomenon."

— Well, that was it, but what did you do after the apparition?

— "First, I thought of Father Slavko. Since I was sitting at the end of the divan, I rose and went towards him. He was by the door and saying to me: 'There! There!' He repeated this to me once more before I realized he was referring to my crutches. I took the crutches and, at the same moment, something happened 'inside'. I took a deep breath, raised my hand to my mouth and I felt like a bird flying in the air! I remember this well. When I passed in front of Father Slavko, he was still at the door and was looking at me in amazement. I told him I would have forgotten my crutches had he not been there. I climbed down the stairs..."

— And then?

— "I didn't know what to do with my crutches. Many people came close to me and took photos. Then I went to put my crutches in the car and entered the church. I was walking straight through the crowd. A few persons I knew pulled me into a pew to ask me again what I had done with my crutches. Only then, did it become clear to me that I did not need my crutches anymore! I was simply walking! I began to shake and I felt uneasy. I began to weep out of shock... The next day, I went to the hill of the apparitions. A young English lady was holding me by hand. On my way back, I needed no help. She could not follow me. On the second day, I went to mount Krizevac. There were three of us. I was the first to go up and to come down. I had neither pain, nor cramps in my muscles, something which, to everyone including myself, did not seem normal. These were the first steps on my own in the last twelve years.''

— How did you understand and accept all that?

— ''First, I told Father Slavko that, according to me, I would have the strength to go without crutches, even at home, but I did not clearly see how all this would develop.''

— To whom did you attribute this healing?

— ''It is not based on any personal effort of mine. After some time I understood that I was being asked only to have a complete trust.''

— And now, what about your relation to God and to prayer?

— ''Many things have thoroughly changed in regard to God and prayer! Something occurred which could be described as a change of 'polarities'. God does not do things by halves; this is why He demands an absolute trust. Therefore, this is a question of total healing, but it cannot be achieved in one go. Everything unfolds at a rhythm known to God alone.''

— How do you now perceive the people around you?

— ''I see that they are in a terrible rush. Why, in general, are they here if they behave this way? I have changed my attitudes towards the majority of people, especially the handicapped, for I always see myself in them. There are many things which are a 'challenge' to me, but I do not speak about this to everybody. Sometimes, I must speak about this to those who need it so that they may not lose their hope and trust in God.''

— This is all very well, Agnes, but you have prolonged your stay in Medjugorje?

— ''I thought I would stay until May 24, but now, it seems to me that I must yet leave something else here. The real reason for my stay lies within myself. I have, as it were, the belief that something else must yet take place in me. And this is in the process of becoming real...''

— Did you get in touch with your mother?

— "Certainly! I have also written to my friends. I have made all this known to my doctor."

— What are you doing now in Medjugorje?

— "I pray, I have never prayed so much. It is wonderful for me when I can manage to hide in some corner and pray. I do not do this out of a sense of obligation, but because my soul demands it."

And so days went by in this way for Agnes and they still do.

At the end of October, she made a declaration to the German press in which she says among other things: "Up to this day, I have been feeling well. As for the doctors, this healing is beyond understanding from the human and the medical point of view. I do not experience difficulties with my legs anymore. Neither do my lungs give me any signs of my former troubles. My memory, which had weakened, now functions amazingly well. For me, this healing is a sheer gratuitous gift. I did not even go to Medjugorje to be healed, but rather because I felt within myself a very strong urge to do so. God has drawn so near to me with his love that I always feel His presence and it is constantly renewed. Our journey with Him never comes to an end... The most important thing for us is to open ourselves to His love.

I am giving this testimony only out of love for God to show to all men His concern about them. I also want to bear witness to my Mother the Virgin Mary whose hand offers us peace."

After this statement, which Agnes Heupel gave to the public on August 24, 1986, there is no need to draw any other conclusion on the work of God and of the Virgin Mary in Medjugorje. As we bring this chapter to an end, we could add to it the beautiful gift of the two crutches which Agnes left behind in Medjugorje.

Janko Bubalo

In Medjugorje, Mary Communicates Her Message to Each Pilgrim

In the course of these last years, everyone of us has heard through the media about the apparitions of the Blessed Virgin Mary in Medjugorje. Like many of us I cherished the hope of going there myself someday. The opportunity came up unexpectedly in October 1986. On the one hand, I had to be in London on October 13 to present a series of lectures on the results of the research of the Interhospital Network of Cancerology of the University of Montreal on the treatment of cancer of the endometrium. On the other hand, my wife and I were to accompany our mother to Alexandria in Egypt. We then spontaneously decided that Medjugorje would be on our itinerary between Cairo and London.

So on Thursday, October 9, on a glorious morning, we were driving on the winding motorway along the Adriatic Sea which leads to this BLESSED LAND of Medjugorje. Not knowing how to reach this land, we followed a bus which was precisely taking a group of pilgrims from Quebec accompanied by their guide, Mrs. Klanac, to this same destination. The amazing thing is that our unplanned pilgrimage coincided with the dates of the arrival of the pilgrims from Montreal. Furthermore, in Medjugorje, I met my friend Father Armand Girard from the pastoral team of the Notre Dame Hospital as well as his brother Father Guy Girard.

How shall I describe the first impressions I had when we arrived at Medjugorje? Medjugorje is not a hamlet, but rather an *oasis of peace* and gentleness surrounded by rather arid-looking mountains. In the various peasant homes where we stopped, we were greeted by simple smiling villagers.

The first afternoon, we went to the parish house where we joined the pilgrims to recite the rosary in the small yard behind the room where the apparitions take place. Suddenly, there was silence and a prayerful calm as soon as a lamp was lit in the little room of the apparitions. This corresponds to the moment the Virgin Mary appears to the visionaries. A few minutes later, we had the joy of noticing Marija and Jakov stealthily leaving the parish house. It was only two days later that I learned through Father Slavko Barbarić the message Our Lady had given us through the mediacy of these young people of this Thursday, the 9th of October. We then attended the concelebrated High Mass in the parish of St. James. At the time of the Eucharistic Prayer, Father Armand Girard called upon us to pray for the success of the International Day of Peace which was to take place under the auspices of His Holiness John Paul II at Assisi on October 24. I then thought of Lebanon which has been plagued by an atrocious civil war for the last twelve years... A few minutes later, I was moved when I received Holy Communion from the hands of Father Tomislav Vlasić, former pastor of the parish of Saint James. Night was falling rapidly. Our heart was filled with all we had seen and experienced. We left Medjugorje to have supper and a night's rest at Citluk, a small neighboring village.

Friday, October 10, was a memorable day during which a series of happy events followed one another until late in the evening. Early in the morning, we joined again the group of pilgrims from Quebec led by Mrs. Daria Klanac. The pilgrimage began by going to the home of Vicka, one of the visionaries to whom the apparitions were being interrupted (absence of apparitions) for a third time. She was there smiling radiantly, speaking to a group of pilgrims. In spite of the fact that she was greeting and shaking hands with hundreds of pilgrims, she did not lose her serenity. After I had taken a few souvenir photos, I asked her through our guide-interpreter, Madam Klanac, what was the most important message of Our Lady. Very simply, she answered that there is not only one important message…, there are many which bear on prayer, penance, fasting, communion, conversion and reconciliation.

Then it was the climb on the hill of the first apparitions (the Podbrdo hill) under the noon sun. When we reached the top, at the very place where the Virgin Mary had first appeared to the visionaries, we could see a multitude of crosses which had been staked by the pilgrims and embellished by means of invocations and pictures of Our Lady. We recollected ourselves and recited together each seven times the "Our Father", the "Hail Mary", the "Glory be to the Father" and then the "I believe in God". Then we sang the Ave Maria. We could feel a great peace mingled with the freshness of a breeze hovering in the atmosphere. Near the top, a young artist was transforming rocks into souvenir-stones decorated with invocations written in gold. These were on display and laid out for the pilgrims. He was not asking for anything in return nor was he selling any of them. He was all taken up by his painting and by the pleasantness of the site. In June 1986, on the fifth anniversary of the apparitions, a beautiful cross was raised on the center of this hill, bearing a special inscription in Croatian which reads as follows: "I believe in the Eternal Light. Allow yourself to be entirely imbued by It. Soon you will all come to Me, everyone from the first to the last. Think with what good deeds you are going to present yourselves to Me."

Coming down from the hill, we went by the home of Ivanka, one of the visionaries who knows the ten secrets, but who does not see the Blessed Virgin anymore except once a year on the anniversary of the apparitions in June. She had the same radiant and serene expression I had noticed in Vicka. While most of the pilgrims were taking a moment of rest, I, with Madam Klanac and Father Armand Girard, went to see Marija who was working in the fields. Marija, who continues to see the Virgin Mary on a daily basis, is different from the other visionaries. She is more reserved and more concerned. All the "spotlights" were aimed at her and Jakov. Meanwhile, she was as simple as the others and answered our questions with amazing candor and transparency. To an Irish lady who was asking her to bless a few souvenirs she had purchased, she replied: "It is not up to me to bless your pictures. Go to the church and a priest will bless them."

It was already three in the afternoon and most of the pilgrims decided to take some rest. At the door of our pension, we met Jelena Vasilij. She is a young girl of fourteen who sees Our Lady in her heart. Mary declared the following to Jelena: "I come to you in a manner different from the one I use with the others, not to reveal things to the world through you, but rather to lead you on the way to consecration and holiness."

At about four o'clock, we went, Jocelyne and I, to have a snack in a small restaurant "La Palma". While I was wondering whether or not I should fast, what a surprise it was for me to hear an old American priest tell the waiter in an accent from the Midwest: "Bring me, please, two portions of bread and water." I was amused and happy to see such faith. That made up my mind to follow the example of the pastor and to be contented with bread and water for my meal.

At five in the afternoon, thanks to the recommendations of Madam Klanac and of Fathers Armand and Guy Girard, I found myself in the midst of a large number of priests and a few lay persons in the room of the apparitions in the parish house. I was greatly moved by this privilege and I was reciting my rosary fervently. A few minutes later, Marija and Jakov with Father Slavko joined us. On their knees, they began to say the rosary in Croatian. In the middle of the third sorrowful mystery, Marija and Jakov rose slowly and took their places facing the wall near the couch on which the different objects to be blessed were laid out. The light was turned on and they were again on their knees, eyes raised up above. Their faces were radiant; Our Lady was there. Their lips were moving, but there was no sound. These memorable moments went by so rapidly that I could not manage to regain my senses. I was there, again with the pilgrims, distributing to them souvenir-objects which had been blessed by Our Lady. Jocelyne and I took the direction of the church where we attended Mass and the adoration of the Holy Cross.

In the evening, at eight o'clock, a small group of Italian pilgrims and some from Quebec were to meet at the foot of Mount Krizevac. Our Lady had indeed asked Marija to go to pray at the summit of this mountain along with her prayer group. Marija had obtained the permission from Our Lady to be accompanied by some twenty pilgrims. The uphill slopes were steep and strewn with sharp and slippery rocks. We made a halt at each of the fourteen stations of the cross to recite the rosary before reaching the top. At the sixth station, Jocelyne began to grow weak and she decided to stop there. I decided to stay with her because we were out of breath and exhausted. Suddenly, a young Italian man of Marija's group as well as a lady retraced their steps and encouraged us to continue the climb. They were admirably helpful and, a few moments later, we were all together again at the summit of Mount Krizevac where an enormous concrete cross overlooks the whole mountain. I have never felt so close to the stars. Marija led us in the recitation of the Rosary. Then followed the apparition of Our Lady to Marija. Silence reigned over the mountain and the pilgrims were all kneeling on the rugged stones. These were moments of intense fervor. At the end of the apparition, Marija informed us in Italian about the message of Our Lady. "The most Blessed Virgin Mary is very pleased with us and with the sacrifice we made in climbing this mountain to pray. She tells us not to be afraid of making sacrifices. She will always be there to help us make them. Our Lady then gave each one of us a special blessing." To me, this meant that She was sending each of us on the mission of bearing witness to and spreading the Good News.

Then came the staggering descent from the mountain. Jocelyne stumbled on a rock and injured her left knee. The Fathers Girard and other pilgrims came to our rescue. Jocelyne told us with a smile: "The Blessed Virgin Mary does not want me to forget this memorable evening for a long time..."

It was two in the morning when, exhausted, we were able to go to sleep in our pension.

On Saturday, October 11, a few hours before leaving Medjugorje, I attended an informative lecture given by Father Slavko Barbarić. First, he spoke to us about the message of Our Lady at Medjugorje and of the five requests she is making, that is:
— To reconcile ourselves to obtain peace — To pray — To fast — To convert ourselves and To abandon ourselves to Her. He

then took time to elaborate on the messages that the Blessed Virgin Mary had communicated to the visionaries on the last two Thursdays prior to October 11. In the message of October 2, Our Lady teaches us the art of praying by devoting the time necessary, by concentrating ourselves and by not allowing ourselves to be disturbed in the course of prayer. As for the message of Thursday, October 9, which happened to be the first day of my stay in Medjugorje, Our Lady let us know that She wants to guide us in the way of Holiness. We shall not become holy by force, but rather by living the traits of holiness: joy, hope and love. The Blessed Virgin Mary asks us to help her by not being afraid to deny ourselves. She tells us: "On your way to holiness, everyday you will find something that prevents you from becoming holy. Joyfully, give up that something. Do not be sad."

For me, this message was a whole revelation, a personal invitation. As a matter of fact, during my holidays I had neglected my habitual readings and limited myself to reading about the holiness of two men whom Pope John Paul II had just honored during his visit in France: the Saint Curé of Ars, Jean-Marie Vianney and Father Antoine Chevrier, both of Lyons. The message of Our Lady of Medjugorje had just confirmed the one of Ars in a striking and personal way: "Holiness is a universal call for our times, a road accessible to all and a constant effort."

Joseph Ayoud, M.D.
Director of the Center of Oncology,
Notre Dame Hospital, Montreal.

Part Six

Prayer Groups

A number of those who reflect on Medjugorje sometime ask themselves and others: "What is the Blessed Virgin doing now in Medjugorje?" If we took Vicka's declaration into account, a declaration which says that the Virgin Mary has never before appeared and never will do so again in history in this manner, everything would be clear to us. For others, this question would be easier to understand if they remembered that, with her Thursday messages, the Virgin Mary is giving a formative education not only to Medjugorje but to all mankind.

We could understand even better if we entered more deeply into the life of numerous groups who pray and sing in the spirit of the messages of Mary in the whole world. But the simplest way to penetrate into this mystery without making wide detours would be to become more familiar with the life of two prayer groups guided by the Virgin Mary in Medjugorje itself.

The Small Prayer Group

The existence of this group begins at the same time as the first apparitions. I slipped a word about this in the book *"Je vois la Vierge"* (chapter 23, page 79). The members of this group consider July 4, 1982 as their first day. On that day, during the night, at Podbrdo, at the time of an apparition, the Virgin Mary asked them to be at her service through prayer from that day onward. In *"Je vois la Vierge"*, it was said that the Virgin Mary had appeared several times to that prayer group but, henceforth, She will appear to them regularly. Naturally, the Virgin Mary was seen only by the visionaries present there, but that did not prevent the other members from concluding that She was there and from behaving accordingly.

Here is how this took place on July 4, 1982. A few members of the group, having returned from church at 10 in the evening, were gathered on the terrace at Vicka's home. They could not manage to agree on certain points. Five or six of them, however, decided to go to the hill of the apparitions. At the top of the hill, while they were praying and singing, the Virgin Mary came. She prayed with them, blessed them and set the day and time for the next meetings. At first, these occurred on Tuesdays and Fridays, and then Tuesday was replaced by Monday because there were some in the group who had other meetings planned for Tuesdays, Saturdays and later for Thursdays in the basement of the rectory.

A few other persons joined the group, but "officially" they were never more than 15 members. One would be inspired to become a member and similarly would be inspired to stop being one. The majority of the members were there since the beginning. Some left and found others to take their place.

The Virgin Mary named no one in particular, neither to join the group nor to leave it. She told them on several occasions that anyone who found these conditions difficult was free to leave, for She is a Mother who understands each one of us. Thus, there were four who left. She was full of motherly care for each member of the group. She protected them many times and gave them the strength to be faithful to the efforts they had to make.

Sometimes, She would simply fondle them. Already at the third apparition, through one of the visionaries, She invited them to come near her, one at a time, to kiss Her. The visionary would tell them, to be sure, where he should place himself. It is not surprising that none of these happy chosen few, then as now, knew how to explain or describe this experience. They all agree in saying that, at that moment, they felt something which is beyond all description. There also came up an amusing situation. One of the members of the group was small and could not reach the Blessed Virgin's face. Then, one of the stronger ones lifted him up so that he could kiss Her. All the group burst out laughing and the Virgin Mary also happily laughed with them.

Although She was motherly toward the group, She held it firmly in hand. She determined the day and the time for the rendez-vous. She would urge them to pray as much as possible for her particular intentions, without ever revealing what they were. Almost from the beginning, She would invite them to three meetings: Monday, Tuesday and Friday. She would ask them to help her with prayer so that God's plans may come true. And when the favor was granted, She would thank them for the sacrifices they had imposed upon themselves for Her. From the beginning, it was agreed that at least one of the visionaries would be present in the group. The Virgin Mary would use that one to stimulate the group and to give them tasks requested and planned by Herself.

This was the source of great joy for the visionaries and for the members of the group who would be there all together. It is not certain that the group could have persevered without Her presence. The Blessed Virgin's demands were not very easy. Always during the night, two or three times a week, they had to go to the place assigned for the meeting, and this in any kind of weather. They practically had to devote a good part of the night to this meeting. They would remain at the gathering for two or three hours to read the Scriptures, pray and sing. These were the days when they also fasted.

It should be mentioned here that a few members of the group lived thirty or forty kilometers from Medjugorje. This distance did not prevent them from being always among the most punctual at the meeting. The tasks were sometimes impossible. She was the one who would determine the place for the meeting, but her motherly choice was not always of the gentlest ! Thus during the intensely cold spell of the winter of 1984, they would go (on the invitation of the Virgin Mary) to Mount Krizevac for the meeting which took place at midnight exactly. The deep snow had covered

185

the road to Krizevac and made it impossible. That did not prevent the group from making the way of the cross and stopping at each station which could hardly be seen buried as it was under this beautiful covering. Normally, at least one hour was needed to go from Vicka's home, from which they would set out, to Mount Krizevac. It was a great joy for these strange pilgrims when they reached their destination, knowing that their good Mother was waiting for them up there to fill them with a hapiness never before known to them. They knew very well that they would not have been able to do this if She had not been there to help them. The visionaries who were present would pass on her encouraging words. She would remain with them five, ten, twenty, thirty minutes and more! One of them, who was older, told us he had never covered his head during the time of the apparitions whatever the weather might be (fine weather, bad weather).

They would thoroughly rejoice when nothing annoying would happen to anyone of them. Days went by! The group was beginning to have a problem; they were not alone anymore. For a while, they would hide at a precise spot, at Podbrdo, but other nocturnal pilgrims soon managed to find them. Now they are used to the presence of other people. It was so on the night from August 4 to 5 of 1986. The moment was solemn. That night, the voice, "which was neither word nor noise", had assembled about ten thousand (possibly more according to some) men and women of all walks of life to prepare Her feastday and to receive Her blessing and Her thanks.

It would be interesting to know how their meeting would evolve. No member of the group is able to describe that process. The reason is very simple. The meeting follows no strict form of procedure. Everything depends upon the suggestions made by the Virgin Mary and the personal inspiration of each member of the group. This was not the first time that the Virgin Mary had asked through one of the visionaries that each member in the group speak to her spontaneously from the bottom of his heart according to the inspiration of the moment. Some members have told us that those were the most beautiful moments of their life. They were themselves surprised by the beauty and the depth of the inspiration which manifested itself at that moment. For them, this was a sign beyond any doubt that they were on the right road and that the Virgin Mary was with them.

This becomes a joy unknown in current life. The Virgin Mary sees to it that some warmth be added in their meetings so that these may not become mere routine. She would tell them to write her some letters and to let all the desires of their heart flow in them. Sometimes, She would tell them to add a flower to each letter. They did so happily for they loved to share freely with their Mother. They would come before Her. One of the visionaries would tell them how to move closer to Her and then they would say some pleasing words as they offered their letter with the flower. At this time, they would experience an extraordinary joy. Then they would take back the letter and the flower (if they did not leave it at the meeting place) to keep them carefully at home. The visionaries would tell the others that these little gifts made the Virgin Mary very happy.

This was really something very special! These letters were filled with burning desires, with thanks and with good things. In one of the last letters, they had expressed "the wish to abandon themselves to the *Eternal Father*" and that had brought much joy to their Mother. They treasure each letter and keep it in their heart. One of the visionaries was saying that remarkable things went on during their meeting. One fact to be noted is that the Virgin Mary never failed to be there for the meeting. Sometimes, She would speak of serious matters, but She would keep her joyful countenance and pass it on to her nocturnal pilgrims.

Not one of them could say that he had had enough of this rhythm of life. This is wonderful when the Virgin Mary is the one giving gifts! We have already said that the Blessed Virgin did not always "spoil" these good pilgrims. She sometimes knew how to reprimand and punish. Once during an evening of prayer at Krizevac, on a very cold and windy evening, they were praying, but they were unable to concentrate on their prayer. This was not the kind of teaching the Virgin Mary had given them. Nevertheless, she came. The visionaries saw her and said that the Blessed Virgin appeared saddened by the poor quality of their prayer. She ordered them, as a punishment, to recite the complete rosary after She would leave. That seemed unbearable to them, but they

187

regrouped themselves behind the cross (in some shelter) and they began to pray. (Prayer was not going well at all.) Decidedly, they could not pray. The Virgin Mary appeared again. Those who could see Her said she was distressed to the point of tears. She made them stop praying and go home. Everybody was unhappy but they had to obey the Virgin Mary and leave. Usually, it was different at Krizevac and at the other places where everything went on happily.

Here is an example of this. One day, the evening prayer was in Vicka's home. She was ill and the other visionaries (Ivan and Marija) were not at home. This occurred in about the middle of 1985. Vicka, in spite of being sick, was leading the prayer and the meeting with the Blessed Virgin. The Virgin Mary appeared and Vicka was making noises with her lips while speaking with Her. Someone in the group found that amusing and burst out laughing. Then everyone was caught up in this contagious laughter except VICKA. Do you think that the Blessed Virgin was going to reprimand them? Not at all! She also began to laugh with them. Something similar happened once at Podbrdo while the Blessed Virgin was praying with the group. One of the members began to laugh without any apparent reason, and laughter spread in the whole group. This time again, the Blessed Virgin shared their mirth, according to the visionaries.

Never did the Virgin Mary admonish them for having laughed. She was joyful when they were joyful. That happened very often, especially at Krizevac. Although it was often like that, the Virgin Mary kept on demanding greater sacrifices like the one at the beginning of the year 1986. It was cold. The Virgin Mary asked them to go up to Krizevac on their bare feet to pray with Her so that God's plans might be realized. They did not even wonder if they would be able to do that. This was the Blessed Virgin's wish and they would fulfill it gladly. When they left Vicka's home, everybody was advising them against doing this, but they heard only the Madonna and that was sufficient for them. They would go up without any light as had been planned with the Blessed Virgin for every nocturnal climb. A dozen of these young people arrived all happy at the foot of the large cross, without a single scratch. In some way, this cross, although it was cold, would give them warmth. The Virgin Mary joyfully came right away and thanked them for the sacrifice they had offered Her.

Thus, this huge cold cross always managed to warm them up!

We have already said that the Virgin Mary being a Mother knew the young pilgrims very well. When winter came, her brave Ivan was not there. And so the Blessed Virgin told them to meet at VICKA's home from ten o'clock on in the evening. After prayers at the church, they would gather at Vicka's home to read the Bible, to pray and sing while waiting for the coming of the Virgin Mary. By observing the visionaries, the rest of the group knew the moment She would arrive and the moment She would leave. At the end of each apparition, one of the visionaries would say "Ode!" (She is gone).

All the members of the group claim they have extraordinary testimonies about the work of the Virgin Mary among them. And it is not surprising (say the others) to see them open out like flowers, all different, expected to produce long-awaited fruit.

This is how they were seen by the group of young Italians, ex-drug addicts, who had come to Medjugorje, accompanied by three religious sisters, to revive their faith and *"their trust in the Eternal Father"*, their natural father having disowned them in most cases.

One evening, the Blessed Virgin urged her small group to go down into the tents of these young Italians to pray with them and to speak to them about their own spiritual experience and of the happiness which comes with these experiences.

They were happily praying and singing. The young Italians were delighted with them; they were crying with joy and definitely taking good resolutions to live a new life. In addition to the efforts already mentioned, the Virgin Mary naturally asked the group to make other sacrifices like fasting and charity by which all the misunderstandings of respective groups can be overcome. To put it in plain words, She was asking them to go without sweets and television for which people of our times are so eager. She was also asking them to limit "outings", the use of cigarettes and alcohol. These are the recommendations our mothers keep repeating to their children; it is different when they are made by our Mother of heaven.

We have given here a short summary of the life of this small group of Medjugorje whom the Blessed Virgin guides and stimulates like a yeast for times to come. No one knows how long the group will last but no one of the members wants it to come to an end. This union in prayer gives a special meaning to their life. If we but knew all they know! They admit they know wonderful things, but they cannot reveal them for the time being. The Blessed Virgin is the one who told that to someone, and they respect Her wish.

The Large Prayer Group

The large group was given this name to distinguish it from other groups in Medjugorje. We have already spoken of the small group which was also formed by the Virgin Mary on July 4, 1982, at the place of the first apparitions. These groups in some way form a whole except that the small group was set up first and, in the beginning, held meetings at a different rhythm.

In order to be able to speak of this large group, we must recall Jelena Vasilij (from Grgo) who, on December 15, 1982, began to have inner spiritual experiences. On that day, she first heard the voice of an angel and then that of the Blessed Virgin. We know that, at the beginning, she was somewhat embarrassed, but she quickly had the courage to tell everything to Father Tomislav Vlasić. This was toward the end of the month of May in 1983. Jelena told him that the Blessed Virgin wanted him to form a group which was to be at Her service, a group whom She would guide Herself in a special way. In this message, it was emphasized that the Virgin Mary asks only those who wish to dedicate themselves totally to Her. She urged more especially the young men and women, given that they are not tied down by family obligations or labor relations. The Virgin Mary said that She would give them one month to think this over. They were free to accept or refuse. However, they had to prepare for this by fasting and prayer.

Already, on June 16, 1983, at the beginning of the novena in preparation for the anniversary of the apparitions, the Virgin

Mary gave Jelena a message indicating the direction in which the group was to commit itself. Here are the guidelines the Virgin Mary gave from the outset to the group.

— To renounce everything and to give oneself entirely to God. At first, She asked more especially to renounce certain enjoyments in order to acquire a greater freedom of mind.

— To live in hope and to fear nothing.

— To pray at least three hours a day. The Virgin Mary especially recommended to attend, if possible, Holy Mass every day. She reminded them that it is important, not only to participate, but to prepare oneself well for the Eucharistic celebration and also to make the act of thanksgiving.

— She asked the members of this group not to make any life commitments for four years, such as to marry or to enter a convent. She very simply asked each one of them to pray and to deepen his prayer. This is the most important step after which the choice made should of itself be the right one. At the end of four years, the Virgin Mary would give them the necessary recommendations and advice.

The group took all that into consideration in a spirit of trust. It is made up of 38 members of whom four are married. The Virgin Mary speaks to them through the mediacy of the visionaries[1] Jelena, Marijana and Vasilij. I have already said a few words about Jelena. Marijana (from Mato) has inner experiences with the Virgin Mary since October 5, 1983. Father Tomislav Vlasić is the spiritual director of the group. The group meets regularly for communal prayer three times a week. The members attend daily Mass except when they are unable to do so. Every year, they make a spiritual retreat and, periodically, they have more intense meetings. On Saturday, the group meditates on the theme of the week, examines itself and makes decisions on the course to follow. The group excludes others. The importance of this wish on the part of the Blessed Virgin was well accepted and quickly understood. Without that restriction, the group would risk being at the mercy of the curious and passersby all the time.

---

1. Jelena and Marijana Vasilij are not related. The two have inner locutions.
— They hear the voice of the Virgin Mary in the heart and they see her daily in inner visions (cf. R. Laurentin, *La Vierge apparaît-elle à Medjugorje?*, p. 91).

This would make its sustained spiritual ascent impossible. Thus the Virgin Mary gives them messages while taking into account the individual journey of each member and of the group as a whole.

From the human point of view, the purpose of this group is not quite clear. We know that the Blessed Virgin demands more prayer and more acts of penance from this group than from the others and that She is preparing it for a specific task. Some people see a new ecclesial structure in this group. For a while, the group thought so as well. The question was put to the Blessed Virgin Mary, that is, if it was the moment to take the first steps to form such a structure. The Virgin Mary very simply replied: "Dear children, you don't know what you are asking, you don't know what the future has in store for you. You don't understand God's plans. I ask you to do whatever I tell you." It is becoming clearer and clearer that at the level of the spirit, the Virgin Mary is truly preparing them for a special task and that this task is intimately linked with the realization of the plans the Virgin Mary spoke about to the visionaries of Medjugorje.

With this purpose in view, the Virgin Mary has asked them, as Jesus did his apostles, to be alone by themselves in order to be able to explain to them in detail her intents and her messages. Observations made to this day clearly show us the following: through the mediacy of the six visionaries from Bijakovici, the Blessed Virgin is presenting herself as a sign for mankind to which a general (universal) call of salvation has been addressed. Through the instrumentality of Jelena and Marijana, the Virgin Mary is leading the group toward the depths of the spirit by enlightening it and by helping it in its *spiritual ascent*. The two aspects are part of the Virgin Mary's program at Medjugorje.

Obviously, the group lives marvellous experiences like those of travellers in eternity who go in search of landscapes of the beauty of God and discover every day new wonders of heaven. We could write volumes on this subject. But for the moment, to enter into such details is forbidden for the Virgin Mary said that this is not the time to do so. Moreover, the profound experiences of individuals or those of the group touch upon personal intimacy and no one can speak of these unless he feels that God wishes him to do so. There is always a certain curiosity present among people. They would like to cast an eye within the group, to know the messages, the experiences... but this is not allowed in a spiritual ascent. One understands the messages only if the soul is ready interiorly. Therefore, the Blessed Virgin does not want the members of this group to boast about the messages but, on the contrary, She wants them to observe a spiritual discretion and to be witnesses by their life.

However, here are a few main elements which the Virgin Mary uses to guide them. PRAYER is everything, simply *everything*. To learn to pray in the right manner and to transform one's life by constant prayer is the essential point in the teaching the Blessed Virgin gives them. The word "prayer" covers here a much broader meaning than the one attributed as a rule. It includes FASTING, total SELF-DENIAL so that one's activities may be imbued by the actual experience of prayer. This means aspiring to be eternally with God and to enter more deeply into Him. Very simply, it means to be in love with God.

We usually think we can easily learn to pray. We can easily learn to recite prayers, but not to pray. Prayer is a continuous journey, an uninterrupted purification and an openness to God which is forever growing. Prayer should bring us to a profound personal relationship with God. Here are a few messages related to prayer in this sense:

— "Dear children, you must understand that prayer is not something to be laughed off. Prayer is a conversation with God. In each prayer, you should 'hear' the voice of God. Without prayer, you cannot live" (to Jelena, Sept. 30, 1983).

— "When you pray, spend more time in prayer, for it is a conversation with God!"

Prayer makes everything become clearer.
Prayer makes you know happiness.
Prayer teaches you to be sorry for your sins.
Prayer makes you open out.
Prayer is not something to be laughed off.
Prayer is solely a conversation with God.

"You see, there are so many souls who would like to know

what prayer is. You know that now, try to pray" (to Jelena, Oct. 20, 1986).

The Virgin Mary teaches her chosen ones not only that they must pray, but also how to pray. She says that many pray, but that few enter into prayer. Here are a few points one should follow:

— Prepare the place of prayer from the outside.
— Stay away from noise.
— Stop work and enter into silence.
— Acknowledge your sins and renounce them.

The Virgin says to confess each sin in a conversation before God in the form of prayer. We should do that as long as it is necessary, until the moment when we have the inner feeling that all has been forgiven and that there remains no more inordinate feeling of guilt. When this goes on in the group, the Virgin Mary demands that each acknowledge his weaknesses in front of the others, that they open themselves in humility, the one to the others, and that they help one another in love and in prayer. In order that the soul may be more and more inclined to prayer and that prayer be lasting, the Virgin Mary recommends weekly confession. This practice has proved to be of great importance. Thus, each week, they can check their progress. They become aware of their shortcomings. They drive away the obstacles which prevent them from growing in love. We have experienced that the least residue of sin remaining in us obscures our conscience and limits our mind. Confession is the door opening out to prayer. We must hand over all our difficulties to God. This is not something rational. This is a most profound act. We may enter into prayer only if we liberate ourselves from all sin. We cannot enter into prayer if we are overburdened by our worries and preoccupations. *We must leave everything up to Jesus,* tell Him all about our difficulties and offer them to Him. In any case, the individual must remain in this total surrender until the spirit is completely liberated.

There is no question here of a sentimental or psychological "riddance of burdens". It is a liberation of the spirit. In spite of the cross lying in wait for us, our problems are not problems anymore; our heart is filled with peace and joy. We can be listening in to God only after we have achieved this openness of heart. When freedom has taken root in our soul — freed from all sin and all preoccupation — then the Holy Spirit can work in us, without confronting any obstacles. Therefore, this phase of prayer is one of listening, reflection, meditation, decision making, and orientation.

Blessing comes at the end. It imbues our decisions. We want it and ask God for it, for without it we are helpless. It is important to receive it in peace and to keep it within ourselves. The Blessed Virgin often drew the attention of the group to this. To receive and to keep the blessing, an inner state of prayerful recollection is absolutely necessary. All these phases of prayer may be practiced in different ways: in silence, prayer in a low voice and singing. It is important to keep in everything the simplicity, the direct approach to God in which the vital encounter takes place. Prayer must always revive a person.

Having the Soul of Our Mother

"This is in itself the goal of our spiritual journey. In the simplest of ways, Mary has offered us her virtues and hopes to develop them in us: humility, peace, simplicity, joy, total offering to God, burning love and perpetual prayer. With such a soul, one can pray. The Virgin Mary tells us that Satan has no right to approach the person who possesses all these virtues. She has also said that if we keep these virtues fresh and intact within ourselves like the petals of a flower, Jesus is the only One who can pick them."

Experiencing God in Nature

This is an aspect of prayer which the Virgin Mary has taught us. She often called us to discover God's creation in nature to magnify Him and to pass on our experiences to the others.

This group lays a special emphasis on the dimension of community life. We know that Christianity is lived only in fraternity. This is easy to understand on the theoretical level. The Virgin Mary taught the group how to do this on the practical level. She encouraged the group to work in small groups and gave them themes to deepen their community life. Thus every Saturday, each one was to choose a member of the group with whom he would pray and share during the week. In addition to this obligation, Mary asked them to choose a more intimate member in the group to be able to enter more deeply with him into spiritual experiences, so that these experiences would help them to accept better the other members of the group.

Conclusion

We have given you here some experiences of the group, a scanty information of what the Virgin Mary is doing in them. We hope to have more clarifications soon. Someday, the group will open up to the world, will speak to us of its practical experience and of the work which will be entrusted to it. For the moment, the members of the group tell us that if we wish to learn something of this experience, we only have to pray much, to fast, to accept the messages of the Virgin Mary to the letter and to put them into practice in joy. Thus we will manage to have a certain inner knowledge of what the group is in the process of living.

Janko Bubalo

The Curtain Is Slowly Rising

It seems that the friends of Medjugorje, and its enemies too, are always interested, and today more than ever, to know what exactly is going on in this small village.

In Medjugorje, the life of *prayer* goes on, as well as the flow of pilgrims. At the heart of the "official" ceremonies is the evening office lasting three hours and for which the church is always full. Even in the daytime, this church is never empty; people always come and go. People seek the Lord. Some stop at the church on their way to the hill of the apparitions, others stop on their way back from the hill to pray, pray and pray!

The Blessed Virgin chose this rocky land to manifest herself to the children of Bijakovići. She still manifests herself occasionally (now that they have become adults) late in the night while everything around them is slumbering in peace. (The daily apparitions take place at the rectory.)

Some people also go in large numbers to the top of Mount Krizevac after a long visit to the church. There, at the foot of the huge cross of cold and grey concrete, they seek the warmth which emanates from it.

In spite of the snares set by men and Satan, this life goes on.

Two prayer groups of young people, with their unique fervor and enthusiasm, enter into union with God by praying and fasting for the final victory of the Good among men. But perhaps the hand of God is manifesting itself even more in relation with Mary's visionaries. It is becoming clearer and clearer that they are playing an obvious role in these events. Each one of them is visibly entrusted with a mission of which he is more or less aware. It is becoming more and more evident that each one of them, in a special and personal way, is taking part in the program of this manifestation of the Blessed Virgin at Medjugorje. The choice of the Blessed Virgin is not the result of "chance". We see this more particularly in the conversation with Vicka. There are things going on with her, more than with the others, that are absolutely interesting, especially since she has pronounced her decisive "YES" four years ago, when the Virgin Mary called her to greater suffering. No one knew this except the Blessed Virgin and Vicka. This did not prevent events and experiences to follow one another in succession.

At that time, Vicka was beginning to have slight headaches accompanied by dizzy spells. In addition to this, there was an inflammation of the joints which subsided somewhat after the removal of her tonsils. But the pain was growing. Headaches and fainting spells were becoming more and more frequent and painful. No one understood anything about this.

People were saying things about Vicka's illness which were perhaps as difficult to bear for this young girl of 18 as the illness itself. Finally, Vicka agreed to undergo medical examinations, which proved useless and gave no results. But the symptoms of her mysterious illness kept on manifesting themselves. Vicka was gradually entering into a mystical suffering and, in agreement with the Virgin Mary, she was not to speak of it. Neither could she reveal her secret to her mother even if Vicka understood all the suffering this meant for her. One day, nevertheless, she "slipped" a word to her mother to relieve her of this suffering. Little by little, people close to her finally understood what was really going on in Vicka. And yet, her words and behavior denied this. She always showed herself smiling. Everybody, strangers as well as fellow-countrymen, noticed this and were amazed. One Italian journalist called her in jest: "Vicka, italianissima!" meaning that Vicka was always lively and cheerful like the Italians. She was not much concerned about her health condition. In some way, her courage was her weak point as her attitude on May 13, 1985 illustrates well. She spent the 12th of May in a coma, but that did not stop her from making in her bare feet her pilgrimage to the shrine of Saint Anthony at Humac. Late in the evening, after having come out of her "sleep", she joined first her prayer group for the nocturnal meeting with Our Lady. On her return home at about midnight, she told her mother that she would like to go to Humac. Her mother was perplexed. Vicka who had stayed in bed all day, who had eaten nothing, now wanted to go to Humac. How would she bear that? For Vicka, everything was clear. That night, she asked her Mother in Heaven if she could go to Humac. The Blessed Virgin said "yes" and that was sufficient. She knew that all would go well. At half past one in the night, she left with her friends. At five in the morning, after she had walked 15 kilometers in her bare feet, she went and knelt down in front of the confessional. Everything went on in trust and joy. The following day, Vicka spent the whole day in bed in her state of "coma".

April 1985 was a particularly interesting month in the life of Vicka. The Virgin Mary discontinued telling Vicka about her life after 825 days of such revelations. What should Vicka do now with these notebooks filled with Mary's life story? The Virgin Mary herself chose the priest to whom Vicka would hand over her notebooks when it would be time to do so and who would take care of them. Then She told Vicka the name of that priest. During an interview with Vicka, she admitted to me: "If the choice had been mine, you know whom I would have chosen?" "It is better this way", I told her. "The Virgin Mary knows what She is doing."

Vicka cannot say anything more about these notebooks. She told this to the priest concerned who calmly accepted this situation. Since then, we are now in 1987, there is no news. Vicka is not worrying about that. She leaves it up to the One who, subsequently, undertook to speak to her about the future *of the world*; Vicka takes notes about this as well (as she did for the life of the Blessed Virgin).

This is all we know. Life goes on and that of Vicka is marked by a suffering the exact nature of which is unknown. She was especially suffering of not being able to participate in the meetings with the Virgin Mary along with the other visionaries. She had to remain practically alone at home especially during the long winter evenings. But Vicka had complete trust in the Virgin Mary who visited her regularly. During a period of fifteen months, the apparition would come at the second "Our Father", when Vicka would pronounce the words: "Thy Will be done..." This is not by chance! No, because Vicka had to live these words constantly: "Thy Will be done" and that was not so simple! In spite of so many efforts, sometimes exhausting, I could not manage to penetrate into the mystery of her hidden life. She constantly and bravely persevered in her silence and consciously left us with our ill-defined feelings (in ignorance).

It was only towards the middle of the year 1985 that Vicka (possibly inspired by the Blessed Virgin) allowed me to have a little glimpse further into this domain of the secrets. I particularly have her health condition in mind. Finally, after a long serious interview on September 16, 1985, she promised me she would speak a little about this. This happened at the beginning of the year 1986. We learned (this could not be hidden anymore) that between the 3rd and the 6th of January 1986, Vicka was experiencing something "special". We already knew that for months, or rather for years, Vicka had been suffering from headaches and fainting spells which were growing worse with time. No doctor, not even the specialists from the Rebro clinic in Zagreb could find the cause or the remedy for Vicka's afflictions.

Vicka was the only one who knew everything, but she joyfully offered her suffering and kept silent. When a medical specialist had told Vicka's mother in Zagreb on October 29, 1984: "Let Vicka do less fasting, let her rest more and let her arrange everything else with Our Lady", Vicka had smiled and her saddened mother was thinking at the time that there was no help available for Vicka. Her mother also knew that Vicka was not praying and would never pray (she repeated it constantly) the Virgin Mary for her health. One particular detail illustrates very well what we have just said.

This occurred on Monday, September 15, 1984, on the day following the feast of the Exaltation of the Cross at Krizevac. In the evening, Ana, Nedjo and Mirijana were seated in Vicka's room while waiting to go as a group to Krizevac for the evening of prayer. The Virgin Mary had told them to be there for midnight. At about 11 p.m., when they were preparing to go, Vicka began to have headaches. They helped her lie down and then went out on the terrace for a breath of fresh air. When they saw that Vicka was not coming out, they went back in to see her. What a surprise! She was lying down, quiet, her face beaming with joy as when the Blessed Virgin was with her. Out of respect for the Virgin Mary, they all knelt down and prayed. Vicka, as never before, was praying out loud. Moreover, she was repeating several times: "Jesus, my God." Near her was her sister Ana. With each of Vicka's sighs, she would repeat "Have pity on her", but Vicka would reply: "No, do not have pity!" Thus, the curtain was slowly opening on Vicka's afflictions. This was especially clear when to the words of her sister Ana: "Vicka, give us a little of your suffering!" Vicka had retorted: "No! I am giving you nothing of my suffering, I would take yours if I could."

After a few successive medical examinations in Zagreb, the doctors had prescribed "remedies" to Vicka, remedies which were only multivitamins. She had never consciously or wilfully taken them because she knew what no one else knew except her Madonna. I also had suggested to her to take some pills, but instead of using them she would give them away to a lady in the village who really needed them. When I reproached her for having deceived me, she defended herself by saying that this was the best she could do. And so, as I have already mentioned, we were beginning to see into the secret of Vicka's illness. Her state of "coma" was lasting longer and longer. These states could last as long as fifteen hours a day, except when she was free from pain, a condition her sister Ana defined as a state of "rest" like the one which occurred on the Blessed Virgin's anniversary, August 5, 1985. This rest lasted eight days. When Vicka was in a "coma", it was useless to try anything to wake her up. She would awaken by herself, without the help of anyone, five or six minutes before the usual meeting with the Blessed Virgin, in the winter at 5:40 p.m. and in the summer at 6:40 p.m.. It was like this on September 17, 1985. On that day, her mother was waiting for her to wake up. When Vicka came out of her sleep, her mother said to her: "My dear girl, why don't you ask the Blessed Virgin to relieve you of your misery at least a little?" Vicka replied: "Mama, if you knew how many souls are helped by this, you would not ask me that!" Her mother simply added: "If this is so, may the will of God be done!"

After each awakening, Vicka looked happy and modest as usual. People close to her were beginning to see through this more clearly.

On November 6, 1985, during my interview with Vicka, before and after her meeting with the Blessed Virgin, I myself experienced very closely what was going on in her. Although she had hardly emerged from her coma, Vicka then seemed absolutely fresh and happy as if nothing had happened. We spoke of her coming trip to Zagreb (in two days) where she was to undergo medical examinations. A doctor, member of the episcopal ex-commission of Mostar had summoned her. At that time, he had the right to do so. Vicka seemed to heed my advice to submit herself willingly to them. When the moment for the meeting with the Blessed Virgin came, there were only the two of us and her little sister Marijana. The meeting began with prayer as usual and Vicka fell on her knees at the second Our Father: "Thy Will be done." It had been so for more than fifteen months. This was the sign of the presence of the Blessed Virgin. Vicka began whispering with the Blessed Virgin. (Everything is recorded on my small magnetophone which I was holding close to her.) The apparition lasted seven to eight minutes. Then the ecstasy came to an end with "Ode" (She is gone). One moment of silence, then the act of thanksgiving to the Lord and the meeting was over. We hurried to the church. Quickly, I tried again to give Vicka a few recommendations concerning her trip to Zagreb. She should accept to undergo all the examinations possible to know finally what this was about. Vicka interrupted me by saying in a clear and cut voice: "Father, there will come nothing of all that!"

To my great surprise, Vicka told me that during the apparition, the Blessed Virgin had told her: "There, today you have completed the first notebook of my account on the future of the world... and, tomorrow, you are going to Zagreb, aren't you?" When Vicka confirmed that this was so, the Blessed Virgin told her: "That is good, you may go to Zagreb, but you won't need to undergo any medical examination." Vicky simply added: "What can I do now, Father? I must obey my Lady!"

After this comment, we went to church. I was convinced more and more that Vicka's "case" was directly controlled by the Blessed Virgin.

Vicka went to Zagreb as had been planned. She did everything to meet the doctor in question. If only she could at least explain her situation to him. She waited for hours for her rendez-vous which had been set for 2 o'clock in the afternoon. The reasons why the appointment never took place are unknown to us. So having completed her other business in Zagreb, Vicka came back home without the medical examination. Things are amazing when the Blessed Virgin is the one who makes the arrangements.

Vicka had never been afraid of her illness. She repeated many times: "I am not afraid of life, even less of death." For her, she would say: "Death is merely passing from one house to another, from a house not so beautiful to one much more beautiful."

Days went by. It is impossible to describe them all, but I would like to mention one in particular. On December 7, 1984, Vicka felt a sharp pain at her appendix. Brave as she was, she did not even concern herself about it, especially that she (wrongly) located the appendix on the left side of her body. She went to church for the evening meeting with the Blessed Virgin. Immediately after the apparitions, she felt sharp pains and she fainted. She was quickly taken to Citluk and from Citluk, the doctor directed her to the hospital in Mostar. Surgery was suggested for 7 in the morning, but those who were with Vicka did not have any faith in the expertise of these doctors. They brought her back home and, on the following morning, they took the plane at 9 for Zagreb. At 11, they were at the Zagreb airport and one hour later at the hospital.

This was a Saturday, a holiday and the feast of the Immaculate Conception. Everything was ready for the operation at 2 o'clock. Up to this point, this may perhaps sound like an ordinary story. Perhaps! But we have written it for what follows: Vicka told us that during the operation, she had an apparition of the Virgin Mary which lasted about fifteen minutes. The Blessed Virgin was encouraging her as She alone knows how to do so. A lady from Zagreb said that the nurse attending Vicka during the operation had noticed that something special was going on with Vicka. For a moment, she feared the anaesthesia was ineffective. But, the Blessed Virgin left and everything was normal again.

After the operation, Vicka was kept in an auxiliary room while waiting for a hospital bed. She was still under the shock of the anaesthesia at 5:40 p.m., the usual time for the meeting with the Blessed Virgin. The Virgin Mary came. They spoke to each other. Half an hour later, the effect of the anaesthesia was beginning to decrease. The person who had come with Vicka from Bijakovici closely observed all that. He and Vicka spoke about this to some people later. This was a heavy day for Vicka but the Madonna was by her side. The surgery was very difficult and complications followed, but on the fifth day after it, Vicka came back home at Bijakovici. After that and many other events, came the days already mentioned, that is, the 3rd, 4th, 5th and 6th of January 1986.

At about 5 in the afternoon, Vicka was feeling that her "coma" condition was coming back. But thinking that she would wake up as usual for the meeting with the Blessed Virgin, she told her sister and her brother-in-law Nedjo to wait for her to go to church, after the apparitions. They all agreed!

However, instead of waking up for the meeting with the Blessed Virgin, she remained in her condition. At 5:40 p.m., the Blessed Virgin appeared. Vicka was lying on her back, hands joined in her own fashion, her face radiant and conversing with Mary. To Nedjo and Ana, both of whom had had a long experience of Vicka's apparitions, everything was clear. (The mystery of her hidden suffering was related to the One who was visiting her everyday.) However, no one knew and will ever know how to explain this "double" life of Vicka: her state of coma and her animated whisperings with the Blessed Virgin.

Vicka told me that for her this was like any other daily meeting with the Blessed Virgin. Nedjo and Ana, out of respect for the Blessed Virgin, knelt down and prayed while waiting for the meeting to be over. When Vicka would wake up, they would go to church. After twenty minutes, Vicka was still not moving. Ana, of whom Vicka will say: "She never has enough of praying", went to church. Nedjo remained behind while waiting for the end of the apparition. Since Vicka was not waking up, he finally went to church. He was not afraid and did not fear leaving Vicka alone. She was used to this. When she would wake up, she would manage on her own.

It was 9 in the evening when her parents came back from church. They were having supper. Vicka came down, unable to reveal anything. Everything had to be secret, except what they had been able to see for themselves.

Vicka had other apparitions during her state of "coma"; this could be seen in her face and in her behavior in general, but that had never happened to her before this day of January 3, 1986 during a "regular" visit from the Blessed Virgin. It was obvious that something extraordinary was going on. The following day, January 4, everything went on as on the previous evening except that Ana and Nedjo were not with Vicka anymore, but there was someone with her. That evening, the Virgin Mary visited Vicka in her coma condition. They conversed for some twenty minutes; this was, as it were, a follow-up of the meeting of the previous evening. On the third of January, the Virgin Mary proposed a threefold commitment to her. She was free to accept or to refuse, but she had to give an answer to the Blessed Virgin on Sunday, January 5, at the latest, during the daily apparition.

Vicka tells us that she was ready on the 3rd of January, immediately and without any hesitation, to accept the Blessed Virgin's proposals, but the Virgin Mary gave her an extra three days which Vicka wished to respect.

That evening, January 5, the Blessed Virgin appeared as usual. Vicka gave her consent joyfully. After 5 or 6 minutes, the meeting was over. I asked Vicka what would have happened if she had not accepted the proposals of the Blessed Virgin. She simply answered that she did not know because in no way could that have happened. At the apparition of the 5th of January, Monsignor Paul Hnilica,[1] titular bishop of Rome, was present with a group of various medical specialists. They remained a few days in Medjugorje to observe the visionaries and to speak with each one of them individually.

They spoke a long time with Vicka and attended the apparition

---

1. Testimony of Msgr. Paul Hnilica, p. 218.

of January 5 when she was in a state of "coma". What a beautiful opportunity! They had Vicka's mother come in and, in her presence, they examined her. They took her pulse, her blood pressure, her body temperature, etc... Then they directed a strong spotlight in her eyes, applied pressure on the sole of her feet, but she did not react. Everything was normal in her except that she gave no visible sign of life.

Shortly after, she was "awake", lively and happy, as if nothing special had happened. And Vicka would say: "And so, that is nothing." What she was saying is true except that the recovery of the consciousness of those experiences was withheld from her, for the one who gives to man the privilege of having extraordinary experiences can also easily delete them.

I asked Vicka if it had been difficult for her to accept the Blessed Virgin's proposals. She bravely answered as always: "Not at all. Much to the contrary, I was pleased to be able to do something for the Virgin Mary." The Blessed Virgin told Vicka that She would appear to her again on the following day, on January 6, at the usual hour, and after that, there would be no meeting until the 25th of February.

I patiently waited for the 25th of February, the day the meetings were to resume between the Blessed Virgin and Vicka. Vicka did not hide her joy either. That evening, she was at the rectory in the room of the apparitions with Marija and Jakov. At that moment, Vicka was especially happy. This is not surprising. They had not seen each other for fifty days.

Those days were not easy for Vicka. In the middle of winter, she had to fulfill her commitment to go up everyday, all by herself, to Mount Krizevac. This was a threefold commitment, but no one knew that except Vicka. We only know that her headaches had disappeared. During these fifty days, the Blessed Virgin had freed her of them because they did not fit in with her other obligations. This was not the end of her afflictions. Vicka well knew that her headaches and all that came with them would return, but she did not know when.

These headaches came back on February 28. Then, all went on as usual until April 23. On that day, the Blessed Virgin again gave her some conditions to fulfill and one of them was not to

206

appear to her for forty days, that is, until June 4. This time, the Blessed Virgin was more demanding. She did not ask Vicka if she would accept her conditions. She simply imposed them on Vicka. She did not free Vicka of her headaches either. Vicka accepted all these conditions without any inner objection and she began to fulfill them conscientiously. I would like to mention here an interesting fact. For more than fifteen months, I have already mentioned that the Virgin Mary would appear to her at the second Our Father at the words: "Thy Will be done." On January 6, she also appeared at the second "Our Father", but this time at the words "thy kingdom come". This was new! There were also other changes.

During this time, Vicka had undergone a second surgery similar to the one of 1984. She had gone to Zagreb on May 27, 1986 in the hope that this operation would be easier and that she would be fully recovered for June 4, the day on which she was to see the Blessed Virgin again. But Mary had other plans. Vicka was operated, more or less successfully, on June 7, on the feast of the Sacred Heart of Mary.

The Virgin Mary appeared to her on June 4 as planned and on the following days, the day of her surgery, June 7, 1986 included. Let us go back to June 4 when surprises were waiting for her. Before her surgery in Zagreb, Vicka was living at the home of her cousin Skender. They had agreed to recite the rosary at about 6 in the evening and to wait in prayer for the arrival of the Blessed Virgin at 6:40. But the Blessed Virgin now and then loved to spring surprises on us.

On that day, at about noon, Skender went on errands in the city. Vicka remained alone to prepare the noon meal. At the time she was cleaning up the kitchen, something shook her and she found herself in the living room without either opening the door or walking. The Virgin Mary was waiting for her there. Vicka fell on her knees, as always, and they spoke to each other. The Virgin Mary, joyfully congratulated her and thanked her for having fulfilled her obligations... She saluted her and She was gone! The Virgin Mary always amazes me by the beauty of her "surprises". She did not appear as Vicka and Skender expected her to do, so that we may understand that her visits are neither the fruit of the imagination nor of hallucinations, but the free choice of the time, the place and the manner of appearing. On the following days, the Blessed Virgin appeared as usual. On June 7, She appeared to Vicka while she was in her hospital bed, immediately after her second surgery.

This time, Vicka was not allowed to leave the hospital right away. On the eleventh day after surgery, the stitches were removed and Vicka was able to return home at Bijakovici. There, she had to remain in bed on the advice of her doctor. In this condition, stretched out on her bed, she waited for the time of Her visits. Naturally, that was inconvenient for neither one of them. During the first days at home, Vicka did not have any headaches. "The Blessed Virgin knows that I could not have borne these two burdens", Vicka would say.

Yes, the days went by with difficulty, for to that was added another affliction, that of very frequent vomiting. Vicka admits that this was one of her most difficult ordeals. The medical examinations revealed nothing and were an added source of fatigue to the point that she could not remain standing and no one could help her. Her only consolation was her daily visit from the Blessed Virgin. Vicka never asked Her to be freed from this ordeal. Vicka describes the interview of August 23 to me as follows:

— The Blessed Virgin came in an unexpected manner and at a time other than the usual one.

— How was that?

— On that day, I had a very severe headache. I spent the whole day with the pilgrims and at the end of the day I was utterly exhausted. I said so to my sister Ana and I went up to my room to rest a little. I do not like to remain with people when I am not joyful.

— And then?

— I found myself all alone in my room, but I did not want to sleep. I sat on the divan, I took my rosary and I began to pray. I had just completed the joyous mysteries and I saw... the Virgin Mary and I fell on my knees. She greeted me and began to speak to me.

— And you?

— What did you want me to do? When She is the one who

208

is speaking, I keep silent, but something unpleasant went through my soul.

— What was this?

— I thought that this was perhaps my last apparition.

— What can we do about that, Vicka? That will surely come about someday.

— I know that too, but it is not so simple as that.

— Good. That did not happen, but what did you think then?

— But I did not have time to think. The Blessed Virgin immediately began to tell me the reason for her coming.

— And what was it?

— To propose a new commitment to me and to tell me that She would not appear to me before the 20th of October.

— That is very well, but we are told that on April 22 the Blessed Virgin revealed her ninth secret to you?

— Yes, she told me the secret.

— I was told that you wept then?

— I probably did since you were told that.

— You likely wept because of the serious nature of the secret?

— I am not saying anything. I think that you and I have learned how to deal with secrets.

— And so do things stand! I am told that on Wednesday, the 23rd of April, the Blessed Virgin stopped speaking to you about the future of the world. She spoke to you about that from April 17, 1985 to April 23, 1986.

— Yes, yes, you have been rightly told.

— Did you say anything to the Blessed Virgin?

— What do you wish me to say? She explained well what She had to tell me, then, She bowed herself out and She was gone.

— Did She ask you if you were accepting the conditions?

— Nothing. There was no discussion. She told me we would see each other in the evening and that this would be the last interruption.

— And what about later?

— Later, I do not know anything about that. I must now fulfill the conditions She gave me while waiting for Her return on October 20 and then we shall see. She is the One who knows everything.

— That is very well, Vicka. Extra portions are being prepared for you (You will have greater suffering).

And the days went by. Vicka was joyfully fulfilling her obligations. Her headaches came on again, but she appeared to be in better health. She was going back and forth between the hill of the apparitions and Krizevac and vice versa. In the midst of this waiting, the great day of October 20 finally rose. Vicka was living it in her heart from day to day. When the long awaited day arrived, she withdrew to her room at about 3 in the afternoon because she had a headache and she wanted to prepare herself for her meeting with the Blessed Virgin. She began to pray with her sister Ana. Shortly after, two Canadian twin priests, two Italian religious sisters and a small group of young Italians joined her. The latter had been at Medjugorje for about a month to be completely healed from drugs and other afflictions.

All were praying with fervor.

At a given moment, Vicka began to be agitated. She noticed three flashes of light which herald every time the coming of the Blessed Virgin. She hardly had the time to kneel down that the Blessed Virgin was in front of her.

When everyone became aware that She was there, they each fell on their knees praying and imploring each for himself and in his own language.

Vicka was beaming with joy. For almost two months she had not seen the Blessed Virgin. Mary was radiant and wore her "festive" clothes which Vicka had rarely seen. This time also She congratulated Vicka and thanked her for the commitment she had fulfilled fervently. She saluted Vicka and left.

As this was the last interruption of the apparitions, Vicka was rejoicing over the meetings to come and which always continue, but in a new manner. The Blessed Virgin does not appear to her at the usual time anymore, but at unexpected times between 3 and 5 in the afternoon when Vicka comes out of her state of coma; she falls back into it after the apparition. Vicka is often alone to experience these moments. However, we see that the Blessed Virgin remains with her for a longer time than She usually did.

To conclude, we could say this: VICKA had three interruptions during which she did not see the Blessed Virgin. Each time, she was chosen to fulfill three conditions. Each of the three times, the Blessed Virgin indicated to her the cause and the purpose of this commitment. Each time, the Blessed Virgin congratulated her and thanked her for the duty fulfilled. During the first interruption, the Blessed Virgin completely freed her of these strange headaches; during the second and the third interruptions, the headaches came on again for a period of time and after the third interruption, her headaches became obviously (and visibly) more intense and more prolonged. Vicka also says that the most painful conditions were fulfilled during the second interruption. (This is probably the reason why it was the shortest.)

After all we have seen, (some of it clear, some of it not so clear), we can only assert this: Vicka will be able (she says "soon") to reveal to us in what these three commitments consisted during these three "interruptions". She will also be able to make known their purpose. Vicka also knows how long her embarrassing "slumber" or coma will last. But for the moment (August 1987) we must be satisfied with what has been told us and have much respect for what we ignore.

Janko Bubalo

A Miraculous Drop

It has already been said several times that the visionaries, such as they are with their similarities and differences, remain the first witnesses of the apparitions at Medjugorje. Yes, they are the obvious witnesses of this extraordinary action of God and of Our Lady in this place. In this sense, I would add yet another testimony.

I would like to give you a brief sketch of the most serene and the most discreet of the six, the young Marija. From the beginning, the Blessed Virgin has kept her in the center and at the same time in the background of the events. Thus, on the first day of the apparitions (June 24, 1981), Marija, not being on the premises, did not see the Virgin Mary. On the second day, June 25, 1981, she did not see Her immediately, at the same time the others did. When, on that day, they ran to be close to the Virgin Mary, Marija, who was with them, was the quickest, but at the moment the others had fallen on their knees in ecstasy before the glorious face of the Blessed Virgin, Marija could see only a blurred image of her as through a screen of light. The Blessed Virgin quickly strengthened her faith by showing herself clearly in all her beauty. IVANKA was the first to speak to Her.

To this day, similar incidents have occurred again and again. Already on the third day, as the visionaries were returning home from the place of the apparitions, the Blessed Virgin kept her in the background, near a pond on the out-of-the-way roads of Podbrdo, at a distance from the others. The Virgin Mary appears to her alone, carrying a large cross in her hands. She says these words to the frightened Marija, words meaningful and valid for any of the apparitions: "Peace, peace, nothing but peace! Peace must reign between God and man and among humans." Actually, this is the alpha and omega of all of Mary's messages. No one was aware at the time that precisely from that moment, Marija was to become the most important of Mary's messengers. It was not long before Marija was offered another opportunity to be at the service of the Blessed Virgin in a special way.

Indeed! This was on the 2nd of August of the first year of the apparitions. Some still remember that. The Virgin Mary appeared to Marija in her home after the apparitions at the usual time of the evening office. Mary told her to gather all the neighborhood in the field near the homes.

"How embarrassing!" thought Marija. "Who am I to convene all these weary people to the specified spot." But she did what she was asked to do in obedience and trust and there occurred this significant warning, perhaps the most important of all the warnings to this day. When Marija, surrounded by all those people, began to pray, the Blessed Virgin came to give an unexpected message. The Blessed Virgin, through the mediacy of Marija, invited all the men and women, boys and girls who were present to come and touch Her. All fell into line and each one came forward to touch the Blessed Virgin at the spot indicated by Marija. And behold, a strange thing happened. In the case of many people, the touch of their hands left a dirty imprint on the dress of the Virgin Mary. When Marija saw the "soiled" Virgin go away, she burst into tears and wept bitterly. One of the more faithful immediately came to her and asked: "What is the matter, Marija? What happened?" In tears, Marija told him what had happened to the Virgin Mary when the people touched her. This man, in a loud voice, begged the people: "Tomorrow, brothers, everyone to confession!" (to the sacrament of reconciliation). The message was clear! It needs no comment.

On the following day, the priests who regularly heard confessions there were amazed to see so many people crowded together to receive the sacrament of Reconciliation. I shall complete this particular aspect of the attitude of the Blessed Virgin towards Marija by other facts. In September 1981, Marija went to study at Mostar. There, the Virgin Mary appeared to her alone, but in a special manner. For months, the Blessed Virgin prayed with her only for the conversion of sinners and for nothing else. Marija did not question the Blessed Virgin and the Virgin Mary did not request anything from her. Marija would return home to Bijakovici for the weekend. She would then attend the other apparitions with the other visionaries. This was different.

In January 1983, the Blessed Virgin began to give an account of her life to the visionaries. It was not the same for Marija. In her meetings with the Blessed Virgin at Mostar, during the week, nothing was changed. She continued to pray. Most of the time, these meetings took place in the Franciscan church at Mostar, in a corner of the sanctuary. She would return home on Friday afternoon. Then, at the evening apparition, the Virgin Mary would give her a summary of all She had said to the other visionaries during the week to bring her up to date. She spoke more about her life to Marija than she did to the other visionaries, VICKA being an exception.

Finally, the choice fell on Marija to transmit the "Thursday" messages. From March 1, 1984 to this day, all the messages except for five or six, have been passed on by Marija. Thursday was the day longed for by everyone. That cannot be explained by chance! Thursday is the day on which God manifested his love for man in a special way. God now makes us understand this love, shows it to us through the messages urging us to come to terms with ourselves, to seek peace and to know better the way leading to the Lord. The Blessed Virgin and Marija were always faithful to this special rendez-vous. Wherever Marija was, at Split, Trogir, Zadar, Slavonski Brod or elsewhere... the meeting took place, the message was given and this still goes on... At present, Marija is fulfilling another task. Since Ivan has left for his military service, the Blessed Virgin has asked her to take his place and be responsible for the evening group. The young people of this group, guided by the Blessed Virgin and in response to her call, sometimes make sacrifices which, from our point of view, seem unreasonable. There are days, for example, when the Blessed Virgin tells them: "Next Friday, be at Krizevac precisely at midnight to pray with me." The group must always be accompanied

214

by one of the visionaries. Now, it is our gentle Marija's turn to be the leader of the group.

During the night of the 4th to the 5th of August 1986, this faithful and homogeneous group guided by Marija was on the hill of the apparitions. But it was not alone. A huge crowd of people surrounded them, people who had come from everywhere to honor the Virgin Mary. Although there are several of the visionaries present in the group, She speaks only to one of them. This time it was to Marija. A priest present on the hill that evening noted the following (O.B. HEKIC): Podbrdo — Medjugorje from the 4th to the 5th of August 1986, between 11:00 p.m. and midnight. After the rosary and the extraordinary apparition, the visionary Marija communicated the following to us: "This evening, Marija said, the Blessed Virgin was happy to see us in such a large number (about 10 000). I asked her to bless us all. For a moment, She prayed over us, hands stretched out, and then She blessed us all with the sign of the cross. She was joyful to see we were so numerous and especially for having offered Her our sacrifices in her intentions. She thanked us for that. She told us that She loved us all and invited us to pass on this love in our homes and to live Her messages. More especially, She said She loved with a great love all those present that evening on the hill. That was all", Marija concluded. This delicate and charming young girl has become a special messenger of the Blessed Virgin; a messenger hitherto unknown to the world.

In spite of all that, the Blessed Virgin has not "spoiled" Marija too much, especially since Vicka has been fulfilling a special "mission" on her own. Marija is at the service of the pilgrims, both day and night. They rarely leave her in peace. Everyday she attends the apparitions. She is often alone, for neither Jakov nor Vicka can get there. Sometimes, it seems that the Blessed Virgin does not treat her as she does the others. For example, she is the only one not to know the date of the great sign which will manifest itself on the hill of the first apparitions. We know very well that from the human point of view, this is not always easy to accept. But Marija is sincere when she tells us that she does not worry about that because, basically, she receives confidences which the Blessed Virgin does not make to the others, but to her alone.

Marija rarely speaks of them. She, nevertheless, gave us an account of a beautiful vision which the Blessed Virgin had prepared for her as a surprise.

Marija relates the following: "One fine morning, I was alone in my room, immersed in a gentle and deep prayer.

— And then what?

— I had a wonderful vision.

— What did you see?

— I saw a flower such as I have never seen.

— Where did the flower grow?

— The flower was growing but...

— What do you mean... "but"?

— The flower wilted. Its head drooped as if it were dead. This was sad to see.

— How was this flower?

— It was white, but I don't know how to name it.

— And then?

— Then I saw a marvellous drop above it.

— Little or...?

— It was rather large.

— What happened?

— It fell on the head of the wilted flower.

— And then?

— The flower opened out. It was beautiful to see.

— Instantly or gradually?

— Gradually.

— And then?

— The vision of the flower disappeared.

— What did you think after that?

— Not much. I thought of it a little and then I went on to pray.

— Did you tell this to anyone?

— Not at the time, but later...

— You said that the Blessed Virgin gave you an explanation of that one day.

— Yes, sometime later...

— During a regular apparition or...?

— No, that was once up there, on the hill.

— Did the Blessed Virgin tell you on Her own or did you ask Her to do so?

— I asked her.

— What did She say to you?

— She told me that this flower was the image of our soul. It opens out in the grace of God and wilts when we are in sin. And the drop is the image of the grace of God. The soul wilting in sin will blossom out with the grace of God present in repentance and in confession. She also told me to live the sacrament of reconciliation in the joy of an encounter with God. That is addressed to me and to all of us, surely."

It is certain that Marija must have lived other similar experiences, but she treasures them in her heart and in her small notebook.

Such is Marija, the visionary who saw the Blessed Virgin.

Janko Bubalo

Testimony of Mgr Paul Hnilica

Msgr. Paul HNILICA, auxiliary bishop of Rome and titular bishop of Rusoda, writes the following:

"After my third visit in these places, I was able to arrange for a little more time to speak with the visionaries and also with the people who live close to them in everyday life. I wanted to examine and understand what reasons the one who talks against Medjugorje and is opposed to it had for doing so.

I am convinced that this is a case of slandering.

These children are not manipulated. They are simple and sincere. I see a supernatural aspect in these events. Morally, they force us to treat them very seriously. Upon my conscience, I must come to the conclusion that the voice of God is speaking with power at Medjugorje. Crowds of people go there to manifest by their piety their profound belief in those events.

Here at Medjugorje, something extraordinary is going on. Although these events are taking place in a country, small and not well known, they are happening within the Church and in the interest of all mankind.

We must not and we cannot take the gifts of God lightly."

Msgr. Paul HNILICA
Auxiliary Bishop of Rome,
Titular Bishop of Rusoda.

(Translated from a quotation taken from "Madre di Dio" — 1986/4)

Prayers

MIRTHA O MIRTHA

Peace, o gentle peace,
be our constant hope.

Queen of the Peace,
accept our praise.
From all dangers, protect us all.
In our combats, remain with us.

To magnify the Eternal Father,
give all of us your love.

O Blessed Trinity, with our Mother,
let us proclaim your Mercy,
the power of your Eternal Love.

Queen of the Peace, hear the prayer
of your children of the earth
beseeching you to give them peace.

Amen

February 24, 1986

PRAYER OF THE TOTAL GIFT OF ONESELF

Eternal Father, my God and my Everything, I renew today the total offering of my whole being with all the sincerity and the conviction of which I am capable.

I abandon myself entirely into your hands. Do with me what You will.

Bind me permanently on the cross with Your Divine Son, my Beloved. I accept, I even ask for all the physical, moral and spiritual suffering which in your Infinite Wisdom you will be pleased to send me, so that I may be closer to my Beloved to comfort Him, to atone for sins, to acquire merit and to save souls, many souls who will magnify You for all eternity.

And thank you, my God, from the bottom of my heart for all the sufferings which I recognize as special favors from Your Infinite Goodness, which You have sent me in the past. I accept, from this moment on, all those You have in store for me for the future. I shall always accept them as great favors from Your fatherly Kindness for His most wretched, but nevertheless sincere, loving and trusting child.

All I ask of You is Your love, Your help and the grace to die a thousand deaths rather than lose You through sin.

I thank You for making me understand all these truths and love the Cross in union with Your Divine Son for Your greater glory and the salvation of souls.

O my God, with Your Divine Son, my Beloved, through the hands of Mary Immaculate, I now commend my soul into Your hands. Accept the Total Gift of my love. Everything is accomplished through love.

Amen.

Imprimatur: The Archbishop of Montreal
October 14, 1981

CREDO OF THE SOUL IN TEMPTATION

Be hence, Satan, you come too late, I belong to JESUS,
I belong to MARY by my priesthood and for eternity!
My will refuses to believe what you are suggesting to destroy me.

I believe in this GOD who created me.
I believe in His Infinite Mercy for me.
I believe in the CRUCIFIED JESUS who has redeemed me and
    who purifies me each day by His Precious Blood and the
    Alliance.
I believe in the HOLY SPIRIT present within me and in his
    gifts to strengthen me in battle.
I believe in the intercession of MARY, QUEEN OF PEACE.
I believe in her motherly love for her cherished child, and I
    take my place in her arms where I will take refuge forever.
I believe in the state of soul You put me in, my God!
In this feeling of being forsaken, You make me journey totally
    in faith.
I accept everything without understanding, surrendering myself
    completely to Your Holy Will on me.
I bury myself completely in the arms of Mary Immaculate like
    a tiny child who needs all the tenderness of his mother,
    meanwhile saying to GOD THE FATHER: "I bless You
    and give thanks to You for these trials I accept with the grace
    of GOD to glorify HIM eternally."

MY GOD! in the NAME of the CRUCIFIED JESUS, through
    Mary, Queen of Peace, if this is Your Holy and Adorable
    Will, grant that I may recover this peace of the heart, the
    soul and the mind!
I thank YOU for this and I offer You all my love'.
AMEN!

July 17, 1985

PRAYER TO THE VIRGIN OF DISTRESS[1]

O my divine Redeemer,
hanging on the three nails of the immortal tree
of the Most Holy Cross,
in the agony of unimaginable suffering,
from Your dying eyes,
deign cast a glance on this unhappy sinner
who lies prostrate at your feet,
to ask you for the remedy to my great need,
in the name of the Most Blessed Virgin of Distress
whom you wished, at the time of your agony,
to leave to us as Our Mother.
Lord, do not look at my sins
which are abominable
and which cry out for the torrents of your mercy.
But gaze upon the sorrowful face of your Mother most pure
and through the bitter tears which on Her
shine like diamonds offered for my salvation,
deign to receive favorably my request
because it is the expression of a tormented soul.
O my sweet Redeemer,
do not let me agonize here at your feet
in the cries of my pain and the thorns of my remorse,
but heed my request so that,
by living in gratitude for your infinite mercy,
I may have the strength to raise myself
from the dust of the earth
to take up my cross and follow the road
to our Homeland in Heaven
where You live and reign with God the Father
and God the Holy Spirit for ever and ever.
AMEN.

_____

1. Our Lady of Sorrows.

PRAYER TO THE ETERNAL FATHER

Eternal Father, my God... my Everything, through the hands of Mary, Mediator of all graces, be merciful to these poor children She loves so much, these poor souls!

And through the Precious Blood of your beloved Son, purify them all so that they may glorify You someday in heaven.

I ask you for but one thing for myself; increase my love for You alone, my God... my Everything.

My God, in your infinite love, protect your Church, the Holy Father, all the priests and the missionaries; give us holy priests!

Eternal Father, I believe in You, I love You and I thank You. With Mary, I trust and I hope for everything from your love.

Amen.

Imprimatur: The Archbishop of Montreal
November 23, 1956

VENI CREATOR

Veni, Creator Spiritus;
mentes tuorum visita,
imple superna gratia
quæ tu creasti pectora.

Qui diceris Paraclitus,
altissimi donum Dei,
fons vivus, ignis, caritas
et spiritalis unctio.

Tu septiformis munere,
digitus paternæ dexteræ,
tu rite promissum Patris,
sermone ditans guttura.

Accende lumen sensibus,
infunde amorem cordibus,
infirma nostri corporis
virtute firmans perpeti.

Hostem repellas longius,
pacémque dones protinus;
ductore sic te prævio
vitémus omne noxium.

Per te sciamus da Patrem,
noscamus atque Filium,
teque utriusque Spiritum
credamus omni tempore.

Deo Patri sit gloria
et Filio, qui a mortuis
surrexit, ac Paraclito,
in sæculorum sæcula.
Amen.

Come Holy Spirit, creator, come
from your bright heavenly throne,
come take possession of our souls,
and make them all your own.

You who are called the Paraclete
blest gift of God above,
the living spring, the living fire,
sweet unction and true love.

You who are sevenfold in your grace,
finger of God's right hand;
his Promise, teaching little ones
to speak and understand.

O guide our minds with your blest light,
with love our hearts inflame;
and with your strength, which ne'er decays,
confirm our mortal frame.

Far from us drive our deadly foe;
true peace unto us bring;
and through all perils, lead us safe
beneath your sacred wing.

Through you may we the Father know,
through you the eternal Son,
and you the spirit of them both,
thrice-blessed Three in One.

All glory to the Father be,
with his co-equal Son:
the same to you, great Paraclete,
while endless ages run.
Amen.

SALVE REGINA

Salve Regina, Mater misericordiæ
Vita dulcedo et spes nostra salve.
Ad te clamamus exsules filii Evæ
Ad te suspiramus gementes et flentes
In hac lacrimarum valle.
Eia ergo advocata nostra
Illos tuos misericordes oculos
Ad nos converte
Et Jesum benedictum fructum
Ventris tui
Nobis post hoc exsilium ostende
O clemens, O pia,
O dulcis Virgo Maria.

Hail, Holy Queen, Mother of Mercy, our life, our sweetness and
our hope! To you do we cry, poor banished children of Eve!
To you do we send up our sighs, mourning and weeping in this
valley of tears! O most gracious advocate, turn then your eyes
of mercy towards us; and after this our exile, show us the blessed
fruit of your womb, Jesus! O clement, O loving, O sweet Virgin
Mary!

MIRTHA, O MIRTHA!

(PRED SVOJOM GOSPOM — HYMN TO OUR MADONNA)

Music: *Georgette Faniel*
Words (Croatian): *Janko Bubalo*

1. MA - RI - JO MAJ - KO, PRED TOBOM NAS E - VO,
2. PRED TOBOM, MAJ - KO, E - VO DJECE TVOJE
3. NEK' SVE SE ZA STA-VE SMJEŠTAJU U JEDNU!
4. PRU-ŽI IZ - NAD NAS SVOJE MOĆNE RUKE
5. NEK' POTEKU RIJE - KE IZ SR - DA-CA LJUDI

1. S O - BILJEM SU - ZA, BO-lo-VA I RA - NA,
2. SVAKO-JA-KE BO-JE, BIJELA, CR-NA, ŽU-TA
3. ČOVJEK U ČO - VJE-KU SUSRET NE TVOG SI-NA.
4. BLA - GOSLOV PROSPI IZ NAD SVOG PLA-NE-TA.
5. GLADNI NEK'SE NAHRANI LJUBAVLJU I MI-ROM

1. A TI IH PRE - DAJ LJUBLJENOMU SI — NU
2. O ČUJ NAS MAJ - KO S LJUBAV-LJU NAS PRI - MI
3. I NE-KA ZEMLJA SVA UTO -NE U BRATSTVU
4. NA-RO-DI SVI DA SPOZNA-DNU VEĆ JE-DNOM
5. PRO-PETI NAŠ NEK' RANA -MA PRE-SVE-TIM

226

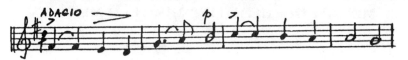

1. KO POKLON NA – ŠIH IZMU –ČE NIH DA-NA.
2. U TO-PLO KRI – LO MAJČINSKOGA SKU-TA.
3. ZAJEDNIŠTVA NO – VOG BEZMRŽNJEI BEZ TMI-NA.
4. DAJE NOVA LJU – BAV U TE – BI ZA –ČE-TA.
5. ZA –VLADA NA – MA I NA-ŠIM SVE-MI-ROM.

1.-5. MARI-JO MAJ-KO!

MELODY OF THE HYMN "MIRTHA O MIRTHA"

CHORUS

VERSE

Music: *Georgette Faniel,* March 19, 1986, Montreal, QC, Canada

THE SOCIETY OF THE HOLY APOSTLES

The Society of the Holy Apostles is a society living a community life without making public vows and in which the fundamental elements are fraternal life, consecration according to the Gospel and apostolic mission.

The purpose of the Society of the Holy Apostles is to awaken and accompany young people and *especially adults* in the vocation of *priestly ministry* and the other ministries in the Church, the sacrament of salvation.

It was recognized as a Society of community life, of diocesan jurisdiction, on the fifteenth of August nineteen sixty-five, on the feast of the Assumption of the Most Blessed Virgin Mary.

THE STARRED SIGNED OF THE HOLY APOSTLES

Origin — A sign of the Revelation: "A woman clothed with the sun, standing on the moon, and *with the twelve stars on her head for a crown*" (Rv 12:1).

A large star — Bearer of a well-known monogram encircled with a crown of twelve smaller stars. The Queen Mary: Mother of Christ, King of Kings, whom she brings into the world, and surrounded by the Princes of the Church, the holy apostles.

The twelve stars — Are solid to express the plenitude of priesthood which the apostles received.

The color red — Symbolizes the love and charity which must inspire each member of the Society according to their motto: "*Above all, love*" (Col 3:14).

To Our Reader and Friend,

This testimony which you have read presented the wonderful countenance of Mary to you. It also presented to you the mercy of the Father, the infinite love of the Son and the power of the Holy Spirit in souls. What God has done here, He can do in you. Be certain of that.

GOD LOVES YOU. Now perhaps you feel like sharing the joy you experienced while reading this testimony. Therefore, we invite you to make it known for the Glory of the Father and the triumph of Mary, Queen of Peace.

You can do so while reminding yourselves of the words from Scripture:

"Your offerings are like
a perfume whose sweet
fragrance rises to God."

We thank you now for your generosity.

May you be blessed and assured of our prayers.

Father Guy Girard, S.SS.A.

Father Armand Girard, S.SS.A.

Address: Père GUY GIRARD, S.SS.A.
Maison Saint-Pascal,
3719, boul. Gouin Est
Montréal-Nord, QC
H1H 5L8
(Canada)